The Wisest Giver

An Eternal Story for all Ages

Diana Diamondson

ISBN 978-0-9983517-0-4

The Team:
Cover Illustration painted and copyrighted 2016 by Sally Rackets
Cover Hand Image is of Charles Hobbs, Diana's father
Cover Design by Susan Harring
Interior Layout by Michelle VanGeest
Interior Book Illustrations drawn and copyrighted 2016 by Dan Rich
Edited by Terry Behimer

Responses from Readers

This story is a fascinating and unique tool for telling children the most important truths for them to know and experience. Parents and grandparents, teachers and leaders will treasure it.

— John E. Best, Cofounder and Director of Research and Exposition at Operation 220 (formerly Exchanged Life Ministries Texas).

The Wisest Giver is an awesome, grace-based allegory. It begins with a community of perfect, loving people but then walks through the fall, salvation, the discovery of grace, and then living out that grace in daily relationships. *The Wisest Giver* is fresh, unique, important, and well worth the read. You'll love it!

—Todd Hillard, Pastor, Editor, and Author of *The Bible in America* and *Take Your Best Shot: Do Something Bigger Than Yourself.*

Dedicated To My Mom

Appreciation

With Love to my Dear Family and Friends

Angela Gloria Bennett
for her life-long love, support, and encouragement

"Aryn" Erica Christina Sollars
for her tender heart that blesses and encourages mine

Carolyn Best
for her years of wise counsel and vital suggestion of "the stranger"

Dr. John Best
for his kind encouragement and commitment to The Cross

Dr. Patsy Totusek
for her caring support and attention to detail

Elaine Korb
for her discerning, genuine heart, and true friendship forever

Judy Adair
for her amazingly generous heart and
assertive truths that set us free

Lynda Hauser
for her insightful suggestions
and faithful G&G love . . . twice over!

Nancy Kelso
for her dear friendship and writer's heart
to give and share so deeply

Sharon Hall
for her beautiful, unconditional love and support
that radiates Christ to all

Special Thanks

With Gratitude and Warm Regards to my new Friends in
the Publishing World

Todd Hillard
for his generous support and inspiring insights
as my first professional editor-mentor-encourager-friend.

Terry Behimer
for loving this story too, and for being far more than a talented editor.
She has been a mentor, manager, guide ... and friend.

Dan Rich
for his generous heart and beautiful illustrations . . .
and for kindly interrupting his retirement to help!

Marian Green
for her sacrifice. I remember.

Michelle VanGeest
for her tireless efforts to create beauty and balance.

Susan Harring
for her tireless patience and meticulous care
in creating the perfect design.

Sally Rackets
for her God-given artistry and faithful dedication
to His message of grace.

TABLE OF CONTENTS

A Note from the Author 1

1 THE PERFECT KINGDOM
His Gifts of Life and Love, Support and Strength 3

2 THE SUMMER DREAM
His Gifts of Adventure, Beauty, and Belonging 13

3 THE WINTER WONDERLAND
His Gifts of Family and Friends, Creation and Creativity 21

4 THE VOLUNTARY DECISION
His Gift of Choice 27

5 THE TRAGIC DESCENT
His Gifts of Counsel and Warning 35

6 THE DEADLY CONSEQUENCE
His Gift of Justice 43

7 THE WISEST RESPONSE
His Gifts of Mercy, Grace ... and Sacrifice 51

8 THE NECESSARY CHALLENGE
His Gifts of Relentless Love and Truth 61

9 THE BEGINNING SEARCH
His Gifts of Seeking and Yearning 67

10 THE HUMBLE JOURNEY
His Gifts of Invitation, Welcome ... and Hope 75

11 THE HIGHEST TRUTH
His Gifts of Free Forgiveness and Real Relationship 85

12 THE SPIRITUAL CELEBRATION!
His Gifts of Victory, Freedom, and Peace 93

13 THE DEEPEST TRUTH
His Gifts of a New Spirit and The Son Within 103

14 THE ENLIGHTENING LESSON
His Gift of a New Identity 111

15 THE TURNING POINT
His Gifts of Wisdom and Discernment 117

16 THE LIVING REALITY
His Gift of Real Relationship 127

17 THE PERSONAL CONNECTION
His Gifts of Love and Compassion 135

18 THE PERFECT LOVE
His Gift of Healing 141

19 THE MISSING BLESSING
His Gift of Understanding 151

20 THE SON WITHIN
His Gifts of Truth and Trust 159

21 THE ULTIMATE GIFT
His Gifts of Living and Learning, Loving and Life! 171

Appendix A: The Gift of Forgiveness.. 181

Appendix B: The Gift of Connection... 183

Appendix C: The Gift of a New Spirit for Every Believer............ 185

Appendix D: The Gift of Christ Living in Every Believer............ 191

Appendix E: The Gift of Questions and Discovery....................... 194

A Note from the Author

Dear friends,

You are about to read a very special kind of story. It is called an allegory, which is a story within a story. The actual story you read is make-believe, but the story within it is full of truth, life, and meaning. So an allegory encourages you to search for special, secret clues that reveal the second, hidden story deep within. You'll find lots of joy and excitement in uncovering these hidden treasures of truth.

For example, people's names in an allegory are very meaningful. When you meet a little girl named Gracie, you'll know she's full of grace and love. When you meet a boy named Colt, whose father raised The King's strongest and most courageous horses, you'll know something about the kind of boy he is. And when you meet Mr. Armstrong, the village blacksmith . . . well, "strong" can have two meanings. He could be strong to choose well and do what is right . . . or he could be strong-willed and choose poorly and do what is wrong. It's the same with Mr. Sharp. Is he "sharp" meaning intelligent and capable, or is he "sharp" meaning critical and unkind? You'll find interesting questions to help you on page 194.

Watch for clues as you enjoy this wonderful new concept of allegories and discover the very special, very true, second story and world in *The Wisest Giver*. Because if you find these clues, you just might discover a third story . . . *your* story . . . the one hidden in your very own heart.

With you on your journey, DD

Chapter 1

The Perfect Kingdom

His Gifts of Life and Love, Support and Strength

Long, long ago . . . in the middle of forever . . . swirling clouds filled the air everywhere. Sometimes they surged into powerful billows of silvery gray, and sometimes they simply drifted in tranquil wisps of white. But they hid all that lay beyond and kept an amazing secret . . . that was now to be revealed.

Slowly and mysteriously the clouds parted, as if by command, and in the middle of the vast emptiness, there appeared a perfectly lovely, brand new world. As the clouds dispersed further, in the middle of the beautiful new world, there appeared a perfectly lovely land called Glory. And as the clouds disappeared altogether, in the middle of the idyllic new land, there appeared a perfectly lovely, little peasant village called Highland, nestled at the edge of rolling foothills and complete with thatched-roof cottages and colorful, flower-box windows. And in the middle of Highland, there appeared a perfectly lovely and altogether delightful cobblestone square.

The early morning sun shone on the square, which was lined with little shops including the blacksmith, the baker, and the clock, soap, and master map makers. The blacksmith sang to the metallic rhythm of his hammer and anvil. The baker whistled as the scent of fresh bread and sweet pastries filled the air. And the clock, soap, and master map maker all hummed at their trades, as the villagers chatted happily and purchased goods.

Suddenly, in the middle of the busy square, trumpets sounded, pounding hooves rang out, and the happy crowd parted as The Great King of Glory galloped in upon His stunning white steed named Gallant. The King reigned in His charger to a regal halt, as the mighty stallion rose and reared high, pawing the brilliant, blue sky. The King grinned a wide and winsome smile, waving a warm welcome to all.

Ah, The Great King. Yes, He was indeed great . . . because He was good. Handsome, kind, and powerful, He often rode into the village to visit His beloved people. And as He smiled, a warm breeze rustled His royal robe and the sun sparkled on His golden crown. His eyes shone with fiery power and yet such great gentleness that the people always loved His unexpected arrivals and crowded around Him to visit and share. He listened. He understood. He loved. Imagine what you have always longed and wished for in the most perfect person in all the world. That was the amazing King . . . in the quaint, cobblestone square, in the vibrant, little village, in the lovely land of Glory, in the perfect, new world.

The good King loved to be with His people and help them. Whenever The King knew someone had a concern or decision to make, He was there. One was Colt, a young, bright-eyed boy whose father had dedicated his life to raising and training The King's magnificent horses, especially the two and three-year old colts who were at their height of power and speed. He loved their brave hearts, strong spirits, and keen intelligence . . . which is exactly how Colt had gotten his name.

On this particular morning, Colt stood outside his cottage alone, trying to decide whether he was really ready to climb dangerous Mt. Triumph for the very first time in his life. The towering mountain to the north looked very different to different people. Some saw its scenic beauty and enjoyed its sheer majesty from afar. Others explored its base for its treasures of healing herbs and fresh spices. But Colt periodically eyed its peak . . . that seemed so exhilarating and so intimidating all at the same time. Which is exactly why The King had come to visit him.

"Are you ready for our adventure?" asked The King. At first, Colt was thrilled at The King's invitation and company. But then hesitation crept in again, unnerving him. After all, it was the mountain of all mountains from where he stood. He faltered for a moment. "Well . . . I, uh . . . was maybe thinking . . . " but he finally just stopped and stared at the ground. The King reached down, lifted Colt onto His mighty shoulders, turned and smiled, and asked once more, "Are you ready?" Colt grinned and nodded.

Together, they left the safety of Highland and headed over the rolling slopes to the beginning of the forested foothills. There, The King set Colt down. Colt took his first tentative step forward, and The King was right at his side as they began the challenging climb. They conquered each cliff and steep pass, each crumbling ledge and dangerous rockslide . . . even overcoming one nearly fatal fall at Risky Ridge! But they finally reached the long-awaited and fought-for summit of Mt. Triumph! It was the best day of Colt's life! And The King smiled.

Then, too, whenever The King sensed someone needing a little extra tender loving care . . . He was there. Miss

Everdear was a sweet, little, old lady. She always wore an old-fashioned, lace-edged cap, and tucked in the lace was a little pink lily that she had actually named Lilly. When The King knocked on her door, Miss Everdear was often pulling warm shortbread or scones from her oven. The King always helped her carry the hot tea and delicious dessert, dripping with sweet strawberries and drenched in cold, whipped cream, out to her cozy porch, and there they would talk until the sun went down and the stars came out.

One day The King visited old Miss Everdear and whispered, "I have a little surprise for you, My lady." Miss Everdear blushed and then grew wide-eyed as The King pulled from his royal-robed pocket, a soft, white kitten. "Her name is Blessing," The King confided, "for you to keep for your very own." Miss Everdear's heart melted when little Blessing instantly nestled in her lap, purring contentedly. And The King smiled.

And whenever The King saw someone in need of help, He was there. Sage Forrester was a kind woodsman and carpenter. Tall and strong, he loved nature and provided firewood and lumber for the village. He was a young man, married to Serena, and he had a quick smile, a twinkle in his eyes, and a smudge upon his cheek. When he needed more workers to build the new village chapel, The King rode Gallant just before dawn to the nearby village of Faithful Falls to recruit additional men. "Our neighbors need our help!" He called out.

The strong men gathered their tools, called to their wives and children, and started out. The whole village of Highland met them, especially jovial Mr. and Mrs. Tidings, the owners of Good Tidings Inn. They always greeted everyone with a good word, good food, and a good time. "Welcome! Welcome one and all!" they called out, and their jolly laughs created a warm and festive atmosphere as they provided lots of hot coffee, cold apple cider, and hearty breakfast fixings for the fabulous people of Faithful Falls.

Joy and laughter filled the air as the children played, and the women chatted happily while busily filling nail buckets and organizing tools and supplies. The men worked hard too throughout the long day, even joining in on some friendly competition to see who could hammer the fastest and saw the quickest. Smithy Armstrong, the blacksmith, was a giant of a man with a massive chest and bulging arms, and he readily won both contests, getting some good-natured teasing in the process. Mr. Tidings, serving some fresh pie and coffee to the men, called out, "Hey, Smithy, let's see how fast you can build me a new smokehouse for the inn!" The men all laughed as they ate heartily and then pressed on.

Meanwhile, Sage Forrester welcomed the boys and girls who wanted to join in on the work too. He gave them the important job of hammering long, heavy planks together to form strong, sturdy supports for the chapel walls. Colt tried hard but kept missing the nail or bending it sideways. Sage noticed and quietly came up behind Colt and gently guided his hand, encouraging his efforts, and soon Colt was hitting the nail straight on nearly every time. He looked up at Sage with a big grin, and Sage gave him a quick smile, with that twinkle in his eye and smudge upon his cheek, and then moved on to help others.

Under Sage Forrester's supervision and skill, the brilliantly designed chapel was well-built in record time. Sage's use of arcs and arches for the structure and bell tower, and his striking, stained-glass windows facing east, would welcome the sun each morning and create an ethereal haven that would capture the hearts of everyone for generations to come.

It was well after dark before the people of Faithful Falls finished and prepared to return home. The men gave each other a good-natured slap on the back for a job well done, and the women hugged each other warmly, promising to visit again soon. And The King smiled.

Now The King actually had another member of His royal family in Glory, a grown Son who was loved as dearly as The King for They were both alike in so very many ways. The Son had the same nature and essence, the same character and strength, the same grace and love as The King. He, too, was great—because He was good. And He, too, loved the people, sharing in all that happened in the village.

When Colt had climbed Mt. Triumph with The King, it was also The Son who had helped by scouting ahead for possible dangers and helping with extra supplies. When The King had visited old Miss Everdear, it was The Son who had called on her too, even bringing her favorite drink, pink lemonade, which little, pink Lilly also enjoyed from a tiny, pink vase kept for just such special occasions. And when Sage had needed help building the chapel, it was also The Son who had labored long and hard, side by side with the rest of the men, until the charming chapel was complete.

And then too, just last year, it was The Son who had been right there that fateful day when the village water well in the square went dry. He quickly led the way, calling out, "Colt, take your friends and run and fill water buckets from Faithful Falls. Sage, gather picks and shovels from the villagers. And Smithy, bring your wagon and horses to cart away the rocks and dirt." And they had all sprinted to their appointed tasks to support the work of The Son.

Then rolling up His sleeves, The Son started digging long and hard right alongside all the men, His strong, strained muscles glistening in the midday sun. Great drops of sweat formed on His brow as He pressed on. The welfare and well-being of the entire village were uppermost in His mind and heart. And eventually, late into the evening, He broke through to a new underground stream and the new well flooded with fresh, living water.

The people cheered, calling out, "Thank You! Thank You!" and "Hurray for The Son!" and "Great is The Son of The King!" How they loved Him! In fact, they loved Him as much as they loved The King! For they all realized that The King and The Son were so close, so united, so attuned to each other in every way, that it was as though They lived and functioned as One.

Yes, for absolutely everyone, Glory was a perfect place. They all experienced perfect oneness with The King and with one another. They all experienced love and relationship that was solid and powerful and real. And life was good. Yes, imagine what you have always longed and wished for in the most perfect person in all the world. That was The King of Glory.

However . . . just beyond the perfection of Highland, far beyond the walls of the village, in the wilds beyond the west gate, a dark figure crouched, barely visible in the dense undergrowth. Beady eyes gleamed and darted about, yet no other movement was detectable. He meticulously observed every detail with disdain as he masterfully crafted his plan. He was eager to carry it out, but the timing was not quite right. He could wait. He peered intently once more through the thick briars and brush . . . and then suddenly disappeared from sight.

Chapter 2

The Summer Dream

His Gifts of Adventure, Beauty, and Belonging

One day, warm, summer sunshine and the scents of phlox and lavender filled the air. The King and The Son rode their stallions through the east gate, Gallant regal and proud, and Valiant, young and eager. They entered the square, surprising everyone with a long row of beautiful carriages following behind Them. The

King invited one and all, both young and old. "Come join Us for our very first *Dazzling Dream Day!*" And The Son added, "Discover with Us the mysteries beyond Mt. Triumph!"

"What lies beyond the mountain?" they asked. "And what will it all be like? And what will we actually do there?" they asked, peppering Them with questions. "Come and see!" laughed The Son. Happy anticipation filled the air as all the people of the village jostled into the carriages and headed north on their surprise adventure. The King and The Son led the way, side by side on their powerful steeds. They galloped beyond the rolling slopes and lush, wooded foothills of Mt. Triumph. They rode further and farther than the villagers had ever been before. Higher and higher they rode, up a winding mountain path until they reached the top of a special peak where an abundant wellspring awaited them.

"Welcome to Wondrous Waters!" called The King. All the people excitedly climbed out of the carriages as The Son accompanied them to the bubbling, mountain pool. As they gathered around, they saw that the pool gently poured an ever-flowing supply of water into an incredible, mile-long water slide . . . made of glass! "Who will be first?" asked The King. Colt instantly led the way, with a surprise cannonball splash that rippled into waves of laughter throughout the crowd. His best friends, Will and Able, quickly joined him. All three swam to the edge of the crystal-clear slide, and with Colt in the lead, they each pushed off, one by one. As they whisked away, everyone heard their fading voices calling out, "It's ab–so–lute–ly a–maz–ing!"

Tingling, cool water splashed on Colt's skin as he floated up and down and all around through nature's sky-blue, fresh air. He circled around and burst through a fluffy, white cotton cloud, soaring with the eagles in the breathtaking beauty of mid-air. The world all around him was so vast and thrilling, he couldn't help laughing aloud for sheer joy! He heard Will and Able laughing with him as onward and downward they rushed!

They rounded the mountainside and suddenly plunged into a dark cave, only to burst forth moments later from another cave just below it, into brilliant, splashing sunshine! They all grinned and speeded downward toward towering green trees and galloping horses and flowering meadows in stunning hues of scarlet and violet and blue. They glided along the crystal-clear ribbon of sheer glass until at last they slowed and effortlessly floated out and over a sparkling waterfall into the crystal clear blue sea to ride huge, golden angelfish and friendly, silver dolphins.

Back atop the mountain, two best friends braved the waters next. Assisted by The Son, little Joy, contagious with excitement, and little Gracie, ever sweet and gentle, waded into the sparkling pool to the slide's edge. They sat side by side, squeezed hands tightly, and took off together, giggling and squealing all the way, calling out, "Wh-e-e-e-!" and "Yip-e-e-e!" and "Splendi-magnifi-terrifical!" Others quickly followed—venturing on the ride of a lifetime!

Even old Miss Everdear took her turn, happily gliding and sliding along in the clear beauty of the day . . . all the way to the waterfall that is . . . when suddenly her little, linen apron flew up and over her eyes and made her scream! The King instantly whisked her up into His massive, protective arms and assured her, "You're safe now, My dear Miss Everdear. You're safe." She was shaking, but she nodded with gratitude as she straightened her little lace cap. Everyone sighed with relief . . . and then within moments . . . they all burst into laughter over the joyful rescue! Even wide-eyed Miss Everdear and wide-eyed, little pink Lilly managed to join in!

The mountain scenery was breathtaking and the sea air invigorating as the people enjoyed the dazzling pleasures of Wondrous Waters over and over again. Others, like Sage and Serena, discovered scenic paths as sunlight gently filtered through fluttering, gold-and-green-leaf canopies high overhead. Colt, Will, and Able explored mysterious caverns hidden within the majestic mountains. And still others simply rested under shady oak trees that harbored sleeping babies, as sunlight and shadow danced upon colorful quilts.

Mr. and Mrs. Tidings relaxed by the seashore, talking with The Son, as the salty waves lapped and rolled.

Little Joy and Gracie built huge sand castles and moats with their friends, even a tunnel that they could actually crawl through . . . to escape the imaginary dragon! The kindly King carried children on His shoulders and in His arms as He walked along the sandy beaches. And people could hear the faint whispers and giggles of happy children as they talked and played in the presence of The King.

Little Gracie eventually tugged on The King's robe and said, "My turn please." He smiled at her, grasped and raised her to His mighty shoulder, and there she stood, high and full of joy, admiring the sea and sparkling sunshine on the waters. She lifted her arms, feeling as if she might soar like a bird, and closed her eyes, basking in the scents and sounds all around her.

As she relaxed, she leaned forward . . . and suddenly lost her balance! She cried out as she fell into midair. Instantly, The King's strong arms caught her and cradled her in safety. He hugged her every so tightly to reassure her and whispered, "You're safe, My precious little one." She rested her head against His chest and heard His faithful heart beating strong and sure. She smiled up at Him and saw her own reflection in His eyes. Amazing love filled her heart and she sighed with a peace that passed all understanding.

Eventually dinnertime arrived, and The King and The Son provided a bountiful banquet table set under a sheer veil with sparkling clear lights. Musicians came out with wind chimes and strings and soft lutes. Bakers brought out golden trays of sumptuous delicacies, sugared sweets, and exotically spiced dishes for all to enjoy. Tastemasters shared their vast array of flavorful nectars, multi-colored teas, and sparkling waters truly fit for The King and His people. And as the evening air cooled, a cozy bonfire at the water's edge provided a warm welcome for family and friends to relax and visit.

As the evening tide rhythmically rolled in, The King talked with a group of men who gathered to hear His always-wise words of wisdom. "Men," said The King, "keep My ways, and you will always know the depths of life's greatest joys," and they all whole-heartedly agreed. Then, as He often did, The King coupled His insights with heart-warming humor. "By the way," He added, "I hope you'll always invite Me along when you do!" The strong, warm sound of men's laughter filled the evening air, and the sense of oneness and community was everywhere.

The King also spent time enjoying the company of a group of women, engaging in their heart-felt conversation and happy memories. Then with a warm smile He changed the subject by asking, "Ladies, would you do us all the honor of choosing the color of the sunset this evening?" The ladies smiled in surprise at the amazing request, and then whispered among themselves. Soon, with one accord, they shared, "We would ask for purple, my Lord, if You please."

Instantly the sky and billowing clouds transitioned into stunning shades of purple and violet, lilac and lavender, laced with shimmering silver and glimmering gold. The children squealed with delight as the adults admired the beauty and glow of the glorious evening. And when no one was looking, Sage caught Serena around the waist, gave her a gentle embrace, and kissed her in the glow of the sunset's final rays.

Then The King nodded slightly, and fireworks burst forth and reflected upon the water's surface, doubling all the glorious colors. Mothers cuddled babies, and fathers cradled little ones as the people enjoyed the magnificent display. And all who desired could dive beneath the darkened waves to see glowing fish, shining coral, and other mysteries of the sea. Colt, Will, and Able dove into the underwater world, and the currents swirled and danced in beautiful, intricate patterns, carrying them along to see many other marvels indeed.

Then as the comforting calmness of the evening lingered, it was The Son who now nodded. Shooting stars spanned the midnight sky for all to wish upon . . . as fireflies danced and disappeared and reappeared in the countryside beyond. It was an absolutely, perfectly glorious, *Dazzling Dream Day*. In that magical moment, The King announced for all to hear, "Let it be officially declared that *Dream Day* will be an annual, national holiday celebration for all!" Everyone cheered in agreement. Then He smiled with a special twinkle in his eye and said, "However . . . " Everyone held their breath for just an instant to hear what He would say next. "However," He continued, "every year I will surprise you with a different day and a different way to celebrate it."

Everyone applauded and thanked The King and The Son over and over as they happily made their way to the carriages for their ride home. The younger children quickly fell asleep, the older ones sighed as they relived the extraordinary day in their minds, and the adults relaxed with deep joy over such a perfect day with their King. They knew they would all talk about it for weeks . . . and remember it forever. Whatever could the next *Dream Day* possibly be like?

Chapter 3

The Winter Wonderland

His Gifts of Family and Friends, Creation and Creativity

*E*ver true to His word, The Good King surprised the whole village the next year, this time with a bright and dazzling *December Dream Day*. Sparkling snowflakes danced in the sunshine in amazing patterns and designs that filled the sky and awed the people, while white hills were filled with happy sledders sliding and gliding in the cold, fresh air. Old Miss Everdear suddenly whisked by on a runaway sled, but The Son caught her just in time! "Oh, th-thank you!" she managed between gasps, but then cried out, "Oh, dear! My little pink Lilly!" The Son quickly glanced at her cap and reassured her, "Don't worry, dear Miss Everdear. She's quite safe and sound." He noticed a few leaves missing from the fragile, little flower, but Lilly managed a weak, relieved smile and The Son gently patted her little, pink-petaled head.

Many other people were busy enjoying the slopes. As they reached the bottom of the hill, lively reindeer and agile polar bears carried them back up again. Colt, Will, and Able eyed the bears carefully for a long moment, then looked at each other and nodded. They bravely ventured to ride one called Roly-Poly up the hill, finding him to be as strong as a . . . well . . . as strong as a bear!

On one particular ride back toward the top, the boys learned *why* he was called Roly-Poly. Rollicking back up at a good speed, he suddenly halted, flinging all three boys head first into the snow! They tumbled over and over until they were covered from head to toe in snow-white casts. When they landed face up, all that could be seen were three pairs of stunned, dark eyes peeping through mounds of white.

And then Roly-Poly did what he did best. He too rolled and tumbled all the way over to the boys. Their total surprise turned into hoots of laughter as they looked at each other. "You look like a snowman!" chuckled Colt. "You look like Roly-Poly himself!" joked Will. "We should have seen this coming!" laughed Able. They all kidded each other as they brushed off the caked-on snow. Then they looked at each other, cautiously eyed Roly-Poly, nodded together . . . and boldly decided to remount!

They were ready for anything now as they held on tightly, but Roly-Poly seemed to smile secretly as he bounded up the rest of the hill, all the way to the very top, without any further incident. The boys looked at each other in disbelief and then burst into guffaws of laughter so hard, they toppled off the friendly brute, into the waiting snow. The good-natured, polar-bear-express-rodeo-wannabe rolled and frolicked in the snow with the boys, then headed down the hill for his next unsuspecting riders. Colt, Will, and Able watched from above. They couldn't wait to see who'd be next.

Other people skated on frozen ponds twirling and gliding with elegance and ease . . . well . . . except for Joy and Gracie. Their dreams of artistry and grace were quite a bit more imaginary than real. But they skated happily together, helping each other along. And whenever they started to lose their balance, The King or The Son instantly appeared out of nowhere, whisking them into His strong arms before they ever fell to the ice. And then with a wink and a smile, He was gone.

Oh how they loved when He rescued them, and they sighed at the thought. Once, Joy whispered secretly to Gracie, "You know, I might . . . maybe . . . just once . . . start to fall *on purpose* . . . just to see Him rescue me again!" They giggled together at the thought, but then Joy reassured Gracie very seriously, "Oh, but you know, I would never, ever *really* do it." They looked at each other solemnly and nodded . . . and then suddenly giggled again.

And, oh, how the children loved to catch glimpses of furry, little woodland creatures peering through thickets and around tree trunks. A speckled fawn wobbled forward to be greeted by the children and a little, black-capped chickadee alighted on Joy's finger and chirped a little welcome to the delight of everyone there. Even a little bobcat playfully pounced in the powdery snow and romped with the happy children.

Joy and Gracie eventually headed to a clearing where others had already begun building a life-sized, sparkling snow castle. They made broad, packed, snow steps, multi-tiered levels, and towering turrets to play games like Hide-n-Go-Seek or Protect-the-Castle! The Son tried to hide in a snow tower during one game, but His long robe spilled out the door and onto the snow-packed floor. The children found Him much too easily, calling out, "There He is!" as everyone joined in on the fun and laughter of it all.

As the afternoon sun sparkled on the spacious castle, The King officially sat down on His officially designated snow throne to officially crown the appointed Royal Heirs of the Day. The King placed His hand ceremoniously over His eyes, and then called out in His most auspicious voice, "Whoever is, at this moment, standing on the top step of the top tower of this honorable and most noble castle, will immediately, henceforth, and forever be officially crowned the esteemed, preeminent Prince and Princess of *December Dream Day*!"

Everyone turned to look. There on the top step stood Gracie and Colt! Everyone laughed, cheering and congratulating them as they shyly glanced at each other. The Son officially escorted them to The King's official throne where they were officially crowned by the very King Himself. Yes, imagination and dreams, love and joy, unity and perfection, all were true, especially on *Dream Day* with their beloved King.

Life was truly perfect in Glory—perfect days and nights, perfect people and relationships, and perfect oneness and peace. Big brothers always included little brothers in their special games and secret treasure hunts. Big sisters always welcomed little sisters to their woodland picnics and special surprise parties. And mamas and papas always shared their love and wisdom with all. No one ever fought, no one ever hurt . . . and no one ever cried. Dreams always came true. Wishes were always granted. And life was absolutely perfect in the idyllic land of Glory.

Now The King had given the people every beautiful present they could imagine, every dream their hearts could desire, and every adventure their minds could conceive. But one day He quietly announced to them all, "I have one very special gift that I have placed on a golden altar in the woods. I ask you to leave it there . . . in My care . . . and trust Me in this matter." The people all nodded readily and agreed to His request without a second thought.

How long the people trusted The King, no one knows exactly. There's no record of it anywhere. But one cloudy, cold evening, a man on a silver horse slowly and quietly made his way toward Highland. No one heard or noticed. No one paid attention as he drew near. No one understood the magnitude of his entrance through the unguarded west gate and into the middle of the cobblestone square. But the truth that would change their lives forever was that the beady-eyed stranger was now . . . within.

Chapter 4

The Voluntary Decision

His Gift of Choice

The stranger entered the square on a striking, silver-bridled stallion. He was refined, self-composed, and based on his jewel-encrusted vest, flowing dark cape, and double-edged, silver sword, extremely rich. As the impatient steed pawed the ground, the engaging stranger asked Serena where the village inn was, and she pointed the way toward Good Tidings Inn. He acknowledged her by a beguiling tip of his dark velvet hat with its flaming red plume, and then made his way to the inn for a hot meal and a night's stay.

Many of the villagers had gathered at the inn that evening, chatting, relaxing, and eating. The stranger smoothly joined in on their conversations with his tempting charm and entertaining stories from around the world. As their innocent interest in him grew, the stranger casually inquired, "By the way, as I traveled here, I saw a stone warning marker along the side of the road and wondered what it meant?" Mr. Tidings, the innkeeper, explained, "That's to warn you to come along this road and avoid the gift."

"What gift is that?" inquired the stranger, but an odd tone seemed to seep, ever so slightly, into his voice. This time it was plump, little Mrs. Tidings who replied. She was quite unaware of the subtle change in the stranger's voice, and always glad to help, affirmed, "Our King is very generous and good, but He left just one, small gift on an altar in the woods." The stranger's dark eyes flashed for just an instant as he asked his next question. "Did The King tell you *not* to open it?"

Instantly, a deadly silence engulfed the room. Mr. Tidings stopped serving. Smithy stopped eating. And Mrs. Tidings tried to steady her trembling hands and serving tray. The people stared at the stranger in alarm. No one had ever asked that question before. Victoria, one of the women at a nearby table said, "I - I think He said not to touch it."

Her husband, Victor, contradicted her. "No, He said not to go near it." Instantly, noisy confusion erupted throughout the room regarding what The King *had* actually said. The stranger just lingered until an awkward silence resumed, filling the people with unmistakable unsettledness.

Then he smiled as he invaded their thoughts further. "I wonder what's inside. I mean, why would such a good King *withhold* something from you, for I can see that you are all good, trustworthy people." The crowd had never thought of that before either, and even more uncertain and unwelcome thoughts slipped into their minds.

In the silence, confusion surfaced in Smithy's mind. *Why was The King withholding something from him . . . from all of them?* But he dismissed it. *It felt disloyal. It seemed dishonorable. It was unthinkable . . . wasn't it?*

Even sweet, old Miss Everdear secretly considered the stranger's suggestion, her eyes glazed over in thought. *Had she asked herself what was in that box before? She couldn't quite remember. But she surely wanted to know now. She could just ask The King what was inside. She could keep a confidence. She would be discreet. Why did it have to be such a big secret anyway?*

Mrs. Tidings kept hearing the stranger's questions pounding over and over in her head . . . until a very unwelcome thought occurred to her. *Could something be . . .*

wrong? Suddenly, Mrs. Tidings dropped her serving tray. Heavy, metal dishes and heavy, glass goblets crashed on the hard, wooden floor. Everyone stared at her in complete silence. She stood there, flustered and flushed, with a confused stare and a wrinkled frown. But she cleared her throat and forced her words to come forth. "The King is *not* withholding anything from us. He's a . . . good . . . king." Yet in her very words, everyone could sense the doubt creeping into her thinking, and then into their own as well.

The stranger eagerly continued, "Surely a gift is meant to be given!" And then he plunged in with yet another jarring statement. "I wonder what The King is *hiding*. I wonder if it's the best, most important gift of all, and He's keeping it just for Himself."

He glanced about the room, then quietly added, "Oh . . . I *do beg* your pardon. I'm a stranger here, and as you said, He has been very generous indeed. But still . . . if He truly wanted the best for you, wouldn't He freely give you the greatest gift of all?" And with that, the stranger sat back, waiting, while the crowd grew more and more discontented . . . and doubtful . . . and then distrustful . . . of The Great King of Glory.

Finally Smithy broke the silence. "I think this stranger might have something here. I mean, his questions seem reasonable and convincing. In fact, he appears to have a lot more insight than the rest of us combined! Why haven't we asked these questions ourselves?"

Mr. Tidings spoke next. He was more forceful. "He's right! I think we ought to figure out exactly what that King is hiding from us! I think we should get that little box right now and find out!" Old Miss Everdear was so grieved, she cried out, "Oh! . . . and I always thought He was so good and kind to me. How could He *do* this to *all* of us?" And the rest of the crowd angrily agreed.

By the following day, everyone in the village had heard about what had happened at Good Tidings Inn and decided to meet in the village square. Amidst the clamor and commotion, Mr. Tidings shouted, "Here! Here! Quiet down! Quiet down!" He waited a moment as the people turned toward him and settled down. Then he continued. "Now you all know what happened at my inn last night. The King has been withholding and hiding a gift from us! And we need to decide what to *do* about it! All those in favor of *not* searching for the gift, say 'Nay.' The crowd stood in complete silence.

Mr. Tidings called out again, "Alright then! Alright! All those in favor of going and getting the gift, say 'Yay!'" Every voice rang out with "Yay! Yay!" over and over with a chanting uproar that filled the square. Mr. Tidings urged the crowd on further with, "Well then, who's willing to find the gift for all of us and bring it back?"

"I will!" Victoria surprised even herself as she called out, "I'll go! Victor and I will go together!" Her husband, Victor, standing right next to her, turned to her in surprise. She had always been willing to help, to volunteer, to reach out to others. But somehow he sensed that this offer was very different from all the others . . . and he felt strange.

Victoria saw his confused look and turned away. She realized she'd been bold and impulsive, but her offers had always been generous and pure in the past. Yet this time, she too sensed a strange shadow clouding her intent for the first time in her life, and it felt awkward and uncomfortable. But everyone else cheered them on, already celebrating the anticipated victory with toasts, boasts—and taunts against The King.

Victor and Victoria were tall, strong, and winsome. They were mature, respected, and capable. They were older and wiser than most of the others, but they had a beauty and agelessness about them that appealed to everyone. Yes, they were the perfect couple, and everyone agreed that they should carry out the will of all the people and leave immediately. Victoria turned to Victor, searching his face, trying to discern his thoughts. He turned to her and as their eyes met, they both knew. They would do this together.

On a nearby hill, the stranger had been scrutinizing the scene when his horse suddenly tugged impatiently at his silver-studded reins. The stranger savagely cinched the reins, instantly causing drops of blood to trickle from the stallion's mouth, choking him into cowering submission.

The stranger's mouth twisted into an evil sneer of satisfaction. But it was not directed towards his horse or the people. They were all merely pawns. No, the sneer revealed his intense hatred for The Great King of Glory.

Long ago they had battled over who would rule supreme and The King had won—until now. The stranger's cunning deception was designed to create an evil foothold, enabling him to overpower and control the worthless people. The trap was set. He would soon sweep the land and rule them all with an iron fist for his own purposes. And in doing so, he would reach his ultimate, all-consuming goal: to crush and destroy the heart and soul of The Great King of Glory. He smiled. This was just the beginning. He turned his back . . . and galloped away . . . in a cloud of dust . . . unobserved. He had now set his sights on the neighboring village of Faithful Falls.

Chapter 5

The Tragic Descent

His Gifts of Counsel and Warning

Together, Victor and Victoria walked out the west gate, side by side, toward the wild, densely wooded lands that lay beyond. It was now late in the afternoon as the people watched them from the village square. The couple hesitated for a moment and looked back. The people waited impatiently until the couple finally turned and again started forward . . . beginning the downward trek . . . on the dangerous twisting path . . . toward the one and only gift . . . forbidden in all the world.

Victor and Victoria walked onward, searching for the stone warning marker that the stranger had mentioned. Victor whispered hoarsely, "Are you alright?" Victoria just nodded but did not look at him. She felt anxious, yet excited too, and that bothered her. Before she could sort through all she was thinking and feeling, they saw the stone marker, up ahead, on the right. Chiseled in the square stone were the words, "Think Again Thicket." Huge, dark, gnarled trees, with sharp thorns protruding from their trunks and branches, created a massive physical barrier, blocking the entire path of the thickly wooded area, a clear warning to turn around and go back.

They hesitated for several moments, staring at the marker, neither looking at the other nor speaking a word. Both glared long and hard at the oppressive obstacle. But as their thoughts raced forward and as defiance grew in their pounding hearts, they ignored the warning. The scales began to tip. Victoria cried out, "I don't care! I want that gift! Come on!" Together, they lashed out, fighting against the tough, sharp barricade. One large thorn pierced Victoria, just below her left eye. Bleeding and swelling erupted instantly. She fumbled for her sleeve to press on the wound to stop the flow. Her wound made it harder for her to see clearly, and that alarmed her.

Victor plunged forward and stumbled, breaking a heavy branch. It created a razor-sharp edge that caught his left temple, cutting him as he crashed to the ground. He hit his head hard against the tree trunk, and the blow stunned and disoriented him. His wound made it harder for him to think clearly and that unnerved him. But a stubborn burst of angry defiance drove both of them forward and they stumbled on. Self-will and self-effort kept them toiling through the dense thicket until at last, they finally emerged on the other side with torn clothes—and torn flesh.

Exhausted, it took time for each of them to catch their breath. Yet Victor seemed restless and anxious to keep going and said one simple word, "Ready?" Victoria nodded, again avoiding eye contact, as they continued farther down the twisting path. Neither spoke at all now. Neither mentioned the pain they felt. Neither asked about the other. Both were preoccupied with their own thoughts, nursing their own injuries, and ignoring a vague pain penetrating their hearts.

Soon a second, stone marker loomed before them up on the right, this time warning them with the cold, chiseled words, "Beware Again Wall." A huge wall, towering and strong, thick and massive, confronted them. They stared as it stretched endlessly to the right and to the left as far as the eye could see. It was overpowering. It was oppressive . . . and it was in their way. Victoria stomped her foot in frustration while Victor shook his fist in anger at the intimidating obstacle, vowing to overcome the seemingly impenetrable barrier somehow . . . someway.

They glared at its dizzying height for a long while—seething with frustration and resentment—pacing up and down, back and forth, to and fro. They searched meticulously for any crack or crevice, any weakness or flaw that could provide them with a way in or through it but they failed. They felt thwarted in their attempts, angry at their defeat, and livid over the impossibility of it all.

Suddenly they stopped. This wasn't just a physical barrier. This was far more. This was an emotional barrier for them—a towering wall of conflicting emotions battling within each of them and they stood in its shadow overwhelmed. Would they fervently heed the warning and return . . . or would they passionately demand their own willful way and press on? It was an intense emotional conflict, an impasse of immense proportions . . . and they both slumped to the ground, drained by the struggle.

Listless and distracted, they each faltered in their own fluctuating feelings. Almost by accident, Victoria happened to notice a small pebble sparkle near the base of the wall. She absent-mindedly reached forward and touched it. It crumbled instantly to the ground. Stunned, she gingerly touched another pebble. It too crumbled under her fingertip. Her eyes gleamed with greedy delight. The scales tipped further. She touched another and another, and Victor eagerly joined in.

Soon a small hole emerged, and then a small tunnel, large enough for both to pass through. They crept through the opening to the other side, rose to their feet, and breathed in the fresh air of seeming victory. Growing more and more hard-hearted to any possible consequences, they ran deeper and deeper down the dark and forbidden path.

Victor and Victoria eventually slowed to a walk . . . weary, wounded, hungry, and thirsty. They yearned for some fresh, warm bread and cool spring water, but there was none. They continued on in uncomfortable silence, no longer walking side by side but . . . apart . . . thinking of what they had chosen and done, and the distance between them grew.

It was dusk now as they rounded another twisting turn and found a small pond of crystal clear water with yet another large, stone marker on the right reading, "Ponder Again Pond." Relieved, they ran over, knelt down, cupped their hands, and gulped greedily. But bitterness assaulted their senses and they spit it out in disgust.

Victoria closed her eyes for a moment, unable to process any more. She dropped to the edge of the pond exhausted. She could feel her lungs heave from her efforts, yet her heart seemed strangely still. When she at last opened her eyes, the final, fleeting rays of sunlight were filtering through the trees. She looked down in the still pool, and her mirrored image—a clear reflection of distress and pain—stared back at her. Startled, she fell back. She had seen a rough, hardened face barely recognizable with its ravaged wound and empty eyes. Victor cringed too as he caught a glimpse of his own raw reflection—stunned by an inner sense of approaching doom. Each looked up and stared at the other with a hard, distrustful glare. Then each turned away.

They did not want to think about what their hardened reflections might mean. They did not want to think about what they had done. They did not want to think about the spiritual implications at all. So they tended to their injuries instead. Victoria winced as she tried to wash the painful wound under her left eye with water. Victor walked to the far side of the water's edge, and tore a few cloth strips from his shirt to bandage his left temple. Each was trying to stop the drops of blood that trickled down their cheeks like tears.

Darkness now covered them as they began to consider the pond's significance. *Could this simple pool actually be a third warning, another supposed deterrent to their pursuing the forbidden gift?* They each looked up at the same moment, as if to ponder the thought further. Gasps fell from their lips, leaving them breathless. There—in the distance, directly ahead of them—sparkled the golden altar, shining in the midst of the surrounding darkness . . . and upon it . . . the gift.

Instantly they both understood. This was indeed the final warning—and their last opportunity to turn back.

The scales tipped precariously . . . and then crashed in the spiritual realm. With willful hearts pounding and defiant eyes transfixed on the coveted gift, Victor and Victoria deliberately made their choice. They stumbled past the pond and onto the final stretch of forbidden pathway. They raced forward—panting and drawing closer and closer—until at last they reached the golden altar, grabbed the sacred gift, and disappeared into the deep, dark night.

And *nothing* was ever the same . . .
from that moment on.

Chapter 6

The Deadly Consequence

His Gift of Justice

ife—as Victor and Victoria knew it—changed instantly and forever in that horrific moment. For the first time in their lives, something suddenly pierced their very being with a violent intensity that shocked their every nerve. Something gripped and shredded their spirits with such searing pain that involuntary cries escaped from the depths of their souls. Something invisible viciously attacked them, demanding instant allegiance and forcing their submission as they cowered helplessly before it. It invaded their minds, crushed their hearts, and so totally contaminated the deepest recesses of their beings, that they were instant captives. Such raw, cruel power—so mercilessly dominating them—was called sin.

Victoria felt a terrifying slashing, a brutal severing and dying of her perfect union with her King, and her soul instantly withered within her as she helplessly fell upon the ground. She could not open her eyes for sheer fear. She could not take another breath, and yet involuntarily it came, and with it another assault of panic and pain. She could not survive one more beat of her heart and yet it pounded again and again and again with the ruthless reality of loss. She lay nearly lifeless before the onslaught, unable to fathom the depths of all that so totally enveloped her.

Victor stood by but was totally unaware of her. Fear gripped every part of his being, intent on crushing him. His spirit shattered into shards of intense agony, broken beyond recognition. The grimace contorting his face gave way to clenched fists flailing against the shocking, dreaded invasion as it crawled into the very depths of his being with a darkness that defied description. Savage winds rose up, assaulting him and lashing his face. Lightning bolted against the darkness that engulfed both them and all the land, and the earth rumbled and then ruptured beneath him with a force that cast him ruthlessly to the ground.

Victoria lay very still—sickened by the stark reality seeping into her thoughts—and devastated by the destructive choice that had dragged her into such darkness. She cried out to Victor to come to her, to rescue her, to fill the aching void, and heal her wretched woundedness. But he did not respond. He did not even look in her direction. He lay engulfed in an inner, raging war that defied subservience in any form and would rebel no matter what the cost. He clutched at his chest, tearing at his shirt and flesh with a desperation that defied reason, trying to rip out the insidious evil that now resided within. In that horrifying moment in time . . . the fall of both Victor and Victoria shook the entire world—*forever.*

Suddenly, a thought seized Victor with a vice-like grip. *He had to hide the gift! He had to escape from it!* "Victoria!" he cried out, unable to hide his fear, "we've got to hide it . . . bury it . . . leave it here. If we even open it, something far, far worse is sure to happen!" He pointed to an obscure, overgrown area. They desperately dug a hole with their bare hands, flinging dirt recklessly in all directions. There they buried it, covering it over with dirt, dying leaves, and decaying debris. It looked so ugly—so condemning. They closed their eyes and turned away.

Victor tried to draw Victoria away from that awful place. He did not know what might happen next and was desperate to leave. But Victoria could not move from the dark burial ground. She stared at the mound of dirty debris, unable to grasp the implications of such a small, simple gift. *How could such a tiny box hold so much power? How could such a tiny gift produce such deadly results?*

Victor grabbed her hand now, and Victoria allowed herself to be torn away from the hideous spot. They stumbled aimlessly, lost in the darkness. Victor eventually managed to identify a portion of the path. They were tempted to hide, but everything in them ached to return to the safety of the village, far from this terrible place. They managed to retrace their way back toward the village. But with each subsequent step, venomous thoughts, accusatory words, and infuriating rage welled up within each of them, demanding a voice. "This is all *your* fault!" Victor finally exploded, half out of breath.

"Y-You should have stopped us—and *protected* me from all of this!" retorted Victoria, flushed with shame and resentment. Victor turned to counter her words with vengeful sarcasm and a biting attack but suddenly stopped. He watched as his once beautiful Victoria painfully limped towards him, covered with wounds and bruises. Her clothes were dirty and ravaged, and her bloody hand stubbornly dabbed at the stinging tears trickling into her ugly wound. He saw in her countenance the depths of her broken heart, and in her eyes, the overwhelming pain that threatened to crush her altogether.

And he could not speak.

It was well after midnight by now as, half-dazed, Victor and Victoria finally reached the village square—only to discover with horror that they were not alone in their devastation and pain. At the exact moment in the woods when they had stolen the gift, all the other villagers had also felt the same excruciating shattering and crushing of their spirits, the same tormenting pain and terror in their souls, and they were all bitterly waiting to attack the two when they returned.

"What have you done?" screamed Mrs. Sharp.

"You're *both* to blame!" yelled Mr. Crafty, and all the others screeched accusations and condemnations too. Victor fiercely retorted, "No! It's not my fault! You're all to blame—every one of you—for forcing us to go!" And Victoria screamed in anguish, "You made us do this! And now look at me! LOOK AT ME!"

But their words were lost in all the chaos and anger that erupted, one against the other. Evil thoughts raced through everyone's minds and cruel words spewed forth. Raw emotions at the core of every soul tore at the very fiber of everyone's being deep within. Guilt pummeled their souls and shame contaminated their hearts. Ultimately, it was the lies—deep and dark within—that seared and paralyzed their hearts, whispering the deceit that they were now and forevermore . . .

unlovable … unimportant … unworthy …
and unacceptable to The King.

An inner war, dark and deadly, engulfed and penetrated their being. Their cord of perfect oneness with The King and with one another had been savagely severed and destroyed. They felt totally alone. Empty. Despised. Lost. Cries and wails of despair erupted from deep within them. Vile onslaughts stabbed at the very core and heart of every single man, woman, and child.

Suddenly another new and unknown feeling gripped and strangled them. It was panic! It hit hard and dug down deep, immobilizing and tormenting them. *What would happen to them? How could they hide what they had done? And what would The King do now?* These twisted thoughts quickly turned in a hideous, new direction. *How could they justify what they had done? How could they defend their actions? How could they rework and restate the facts to their own advantage?* Smithy hesitated. "M-Maybe we could just *deny* we did it." They considered that briefly but then everyone dismissed the idea. The King always knew everything.

Mr. Tidings had another idea. "We could *excuse* our actions. After all, it was the stranger who tempted and tricked us. So it's not really our fault." That sounded quite convincing for several moments. But then everyone shook their heads and dismissed that too. Though no one said a word, they all knew in the depths of their hearts that they were responsible for what they had chosen and done.

In the end, Victor had the answer. "Let's *blame* The King! He was the One who put the gift there in the first place! This is all His fault for not giving it to us right at the beginning! Blame Him! Ignore Him! Reject Him!" Victor shouted. Everyone eagerly agreed, relieved to have an answer, any answer that gave them a way out. They did not realize that their solution exposed the ugly darkness that had already gripped their souls. Yes, they would blame and reject The Great, Wise, and Good King of Glory. Victor began chanting over and over and everyone else joined in too, shouting:

"I will live my life myself.
I will meet my needs myself.
I will live without The King!
I will live my life myself.
I will meet my needs myself.
I will live without The King!"

Pride, however, eventually gave way to secret shame and rejection. The chanting slowly faded away, and the people silently separated and retreated from the dark village square. Inner defeat weighed heavily on every heart, and they all wanted to hide—somewhere, anywhere—deep within the cloaking darkness. Colt stole away home all alone. Sage and Serena ambled toward their lifeless cottage. And frail, Miss Everdear wandered home, silently wiping away stubborn tears that refused to stop trickling down her old, wrinkled cheeks. Yet no one even considered admitting the truth. No, it seemed easier to just leave. Easier to ignore and avoid the whole, ugly mess. Easier to blame someone else and walk away.

Chapter 7

The Wisest Response

His Gifts of Mercy, Grace ... and Sacrifice

he wise King knew instantly what the people had chosen and done for He knew all things. His grief-stricken heart and tortured eyes revealed the devastating pain He felt deep within. He also grieved for His people because He knew the ominous consequences of their choices. Based on the deep, eternal truths of Life and Justice established before time ever began, the people's distrust, dishonor, and disobedience to The King destroyed the perfect relationship they had always enjoyed with Him and with one another. It also crushed their spirits—the very essence of their beings—beyond repair.

In all the world,
their perfect relationships
and their spiritual identity
were the two most treasured riches in all of life itself.

And the terrible consequence for destroying
such gifts—was death.

Yet even through all of this, The King still loved His people as completely and perfectly as He did before. They did not yet understand the depth of His love, or the power of His love, or the long-suffering of His never-failing love for each and every one of them. Ever true to His goodness, The King had a plan to rescue and restore them to Himself. And so the very next day, and every day that followed, He reached out to every man, woman, and child in the village, offering forgiveness and grace, compassion and mercy . . . forever . . . to whoever would come. But they would not listen.

The King knocked on cottage doors. He sent letters by special messengers. He even rode Gallant into the square, smiling, waving, and calling out warm greetings to everyone in the marketplace, like He'd done countless times before, but now they ignored Him. Colt hung his head and ran from Him. Sage deliberately turned away. And old Miss Everdear peered out at The King . . . and then slowly closed her old front door.

The King wanted to help Colt. He wanted to support Sage. He wanted to visit with old Miss Everdear again. But Mr. Sharp glared at The King and spit on the ground. Mr. Crafty scowled at The King and shouted, "Leave us alone!" And Mr. Simpleton actually picked up stones and threw them at The Great King of Glory! The King stood His ground as Gallant reared high with mane flowing and eyes ablaze, eager to charge, but strong, wise hands restrained him. But the three men saw the fiery look in The King's eyes and slowly backed away.

The people realized that nothing was the same without The King in their lives, but guilt and shame kept them far, far from Him. Some people still tried to do good things on their own, but it never brought the perfect peace and joy they had experienced in the presence of The King. It never satisfied the longing that disturbed their hearts. It never filled the vague emptiness that now tainted their lives. Every effort still left them isolated from The King and incomplete in their relationships with one another. It was all deeply troubling.

Still, Colt tried. He worked for Mrs. Tidings, gathering firewood for the inn. But instead of a pure motive and free heart to give, he now secretly and desperately needed acceptance and turned to performing and self-effort to get it. He felt worthless and rejected deep inside and needed to prove himself, so he worked extra hard to earn it.

One afternoon, as Colt entered Mrs. Tidings' kitchen with an armload of wood, he stumbled. The logs tumbled onto the kitchen floor and a few rolled into the coals on the hearth causing a sudden burst of flames. Though there was no damage, a startled Mrs. Tidings turned on him, slapped his face, and screamed, "Colt, you clumsy, stupid boy! I can't stand you coming around here anymore! You're worthless, Colt. I tell you you're good for absolutely nothing! Now, you get . . . or I'll call the Constable on you!"

Colt ran off, stunned and ashamed. Her rantings trailed after him, and his cheek burned from the harsh blow. But it was her condemning words that haunted him most. She knew he was worthless and she had told him so. And it was this that clawed at his heart and wounded him in ways he could not understand.

Sage tried to help others too. He was good at problem solving. When Mrs. Armstrong asked him how she could get Smithy to make her a new set of metal kitchen utensils, Sage said, "Leave it to me." He meandered over to Smithy's blacksmith shop for a little visit, and Mrs. Armstrong had her new utensils the next day. "However did you manage it?" she asked Sage at the square. He smiled and said, "I promised him you'd use your new flipper to make him flapjacks! He'd wondered why you hadn't made them lately!" They both laughed as she headed to the market for flour—and as a glimmer of pride shone in Sage's eyes.

Sage was good with advice too. When Colt lost his job at Mrs. Tidings and asked Sage what he should do, Sage was quiet for a moment and then said, "Colt, what do you like most?" Colt instantly replied, "I love the woods, just like you do." Sage replied, "Well then, I've heard that a dependable messenger is needed to carry mail through the forest between the villages of Highland and Faithful Falls. You'd love the long walks and you're fast!" Colt landed the job that day, and as he thanked Sage over and over—a glimmer of pride again appeared in Sage's eyes.

And of course Sage was glad to help old Miss Everdear too. She had called on him to take down an old tree that was tipping and tottering onto her roof. It was a tricky job, but he managed to fell the tree, root out the trunk, and plant a pretty, new sapling in its place. "Oh, I feel, so much safer now. What wonderful work you do!" cooed old Miss Everdear. Even little, pink Lilly sighed at the handsome woodsman. Sage looked the same on the outside, right down to the little smudge upon his cheek . . . but inside he was different. He charged Miss Everdear a little extra, figuring she wouldn't notice . . . and she didn't. He took the money, unable to look her in the eye, mumbled a quick goodbye, and left.

Even Joy and Gracie hurt each other. At recess one day, Joy decided to ignore Gracie—just because she felt like it. She snubbed Gracie and walked over and played with Prudence on the school swings instead. Gracie was crushed . . . and jealous. She sat alone on the school steps watching them from afar, nursing the growing wound in her heart.

Then she had an idea. "Oh, Able," she called coyly, "would you wade with me in the stream so I don't trip and fall?" Able was thrilled—ready, willing, and able to keep Gracie company—tripping over his own feet to walk beside her. As they headed toward the water, hand in hand, Gracie glanced over her shoulder to make delightfully sure that Joy was jealous too. A few days later, the two girls slowly started talking to one another again. After all, they were best friends. But the wrong was never addressed and it hurt their hearts.

And Mr. Sharp . . . well, everyone just stayed as far away from him as they possibly could. Every back-biting and back-stabbing word he spoke was harsh, every encounter with others was vicious, and he caused much harm to the poor people of Highland.

The people were experiencing what a broken relationship and a broken spirit felt and looked like day after day. It was empty. It was painful. And it was a stark and constant contrast to the loving, beautiful life they had experienced with The King. Yet shame, guilt, and pride shackled them, and their hearts grew harder and colder. It was desperately sad but true—Glory had lost its glory.

And so the day came—that particularly and profoundly important day—when The Son appeared before The King to present Himself as the next step in the great, eternal plan of The King. The Son was always faithful to do what the wise King asked Him to do and to say what the wise King asked Him to say. He looked long and lovingly into The King's grieving eyes and then solemnly sought The King's permission to proceed. The King gave a hesitant but determined nod. The Son silently acknowledged Him, and with that exchange, His destiny was set. The King agonized as His only, unique, and beloved Son deliberately turned and headed toward the broken village of Highland, to try to win back the broken hearts of the desperately broken people.

The Son soon entered the village square, and word quickly spread that He had arrived. People peered suspiciously from around corners, scoffed at His welcome, but eventually assembled to hear what He had to say. The Son felt their resistance and coldness. Yet He willingly began to share the message of The King, for He knew only such truths could set them free.

The Son called out loud and clear for all to hear. "Hear ye, hear ye! The King has sent Me to tell you that despite all that has happened, His relentless love for you remains eternally the same. He desires to forgive you and restore your relationship with Him." The people were uncomfortable, not wanting to acknowledge their wrongs, not wanting to see and hear what they desperately needed to see and hear.

The Son continued. "He invites you to come to Him. His love is ever patient and kind. He is not angry nor does He hold a grudge against wrongs." The people grew more agitated, more defensive, even hostile to His words. They refused to admit their sin, and their hardened hearts resisted Him all the more.

The Son sensed their opposition but pressed on. "He does not rejoice in wrong but rejoices in the truth. He bears all things, believes all things, hopes all things, and endures all things. His love for you never fails!" At that, the people could stand it no longer! Guilt branded their hearts. Pride blinded their minds. And darkness corrupted their souls. They had to stop the words they could not bear to hear—words that reminded them of what they had done—words that reminded them of all they had lost. They had to stop Him. They had to silence Him. They had to destroy The Son!

The outraged people grabbed The Son they had known and loved, The Son who had always given His all for them, The Son of The King of Glory. They beat Him and lashed Him mercilessly. They cut Him and wounded Him violently. They dragged Him through the square to the outskirts of the village. They attacked Him with spikes and thorns and spear. They shamed and ridiculed Him and spit in His face. Heavy darkness enveloped them and their whole world and yet they continued on, taunting Him, mocking Him, and leaving Him in agony . . . until they were sure He was dead. And then they buried Him in a dark, cold cave—and heartlessly walked away.

The King knew instantly all that His people had done. Sitting alone on His castle throne, He tore His regal robes with tormenting grief. Devastating pain crushed His great heart, as the gravest of all agonies seized Him. Pounding waves of torment relentlessly beat against Him, and His anguished cries echoed in the empty castle halls. They were His own people—but they refused His every offer. They were His own people—but they refused to accept Him and His love. They were His own people—yet they viciously killed His one and only, dearly beloved Son—and cruelly turned away.

And so . . . it was time.

Chapter 8

The Necessary Challenge

His Gifts of Relentless Love and Truth

The next morning, the day dawned, or rather it should be said that the day came. But the sun did not. There was a somber, gray dullness everywhere. The people could barely see around them and in no way could you say it was light or bright or warm or welcoming.

It was as if everyone was trying to see in a great, gray cloud or fog. It wasn't the normal kind of morning mistiness that the sun melts away by mid-day. No, this was a disconcerting and unnerving kind of grayness. Something they could almost feel wrapping itself around them, something empty and lifeless and sad.

"Very strange. Nothing like I've ever seen before," said old Mr. Leary. Always cautious and hesitant, he was one of many of the villagers peering from their front doors. Mrs. Leary stood beside him, watching and nodding but saying nothing. Her mouth was curved downward in a tight, little frown as her hands gripped her old, brown broom.

Both of them always kept to themselves. He constantly warned all the children to stay off his grass and out of his yard and away from his garden, and she always avoided even the simplest neighborly chats, staying within the four walls of their home. They both tried to shrug off the strange gray dullness that was all around them—but it hovered around, relentless and daunting.

Other villagers stood at their front doors too, or stared from their little cottage windows. The uncomfortable unknown kept everyone indoors that day, including the children. Old Mr. Hopewell, the village mayor, carried a lantern and walked through the village hesitantly calling out, "It's alright. It's alright. Light your lamps and candles. All will be well tomorrow . . . all will be well." He stopped for a moment at old Miss Everdear's front door, patted her hand, and managed a weak smile, but his voice made her and all the other villagers even more uneasy because in their hearts they also knew that something was definitely wrong.

But no one would admit their troubled thoughts or feelings, and it occurred to no one to ask The King what was happening. How He longed for them to ask Him, but they did not. And so the people lived out that long day in dark, gray dullness.

As time went on, The King looked out on His sunless kingdom. It continued to be gray and dull, and now added to it, was a chilling, frosty coldness. Every thing and every one felt it. The houses were cold, the animals were cold, and the people were cold. It wasn't the normal cold experienced on a windy, wintery day. No, it was a strange, soul-crushing cold that affected their very being, deep inside, and though no one would say so, they all sensed its chilling effect on each and every one of them.

Two little sisters, Caring Christina and Gentle Gloria, peered out the window of their dark, chilly cottage toward their barn. They looked at each other and instantly thought of their poor, little pet lamb. They searched around their simple home for their colorful, old, family quilt and located it under the staircase.

Shaking and shivering, they made their way in the dark to their old barn to find poor Purity huddled in the corner, frightened and quivering. They ran to her and wrapped her tightly in the warm, multi-colored quilt, and then both of them hugged Purity for a long time, rocking her and whispering, "It's okay . . . it's okay . . . we're here . . . we're here." And in the long, empty silence that ensued, they watched as lonely puffs of white breath disappeared into the cold, dark air.

Everyone in the village refused to speak of their problems and continued on as best they could, hiding their concerns and frustrations. No one would admit their need. No one would look at the truth. No one would even consider inquiring of The King. And so He stood alone, on His balcony, watching His beloved people from afar.

As more time passed, the gray dullness and the bitter cold continued, and now a dry barrenness engulfed everything far and wide. The land was parched. The landscape was brown. Even the strong, old oaks withered under the desolate conditions. It was as if a drought-like dryness was draining the very life out of every living thing, including the people. They were now not only alarmed—they were afraid.

Mr. Crafty secretly started diverting some of the river water from Mr. Simpleton's property onto his own to protect his crops. Mrs. Tidings openly began condemning Mr. Sharp for raising market prices to pad his own pocket. And even old Miss Everdear—growing more and more suspicious and critical of everyone—sadly steeped tea for one . . . and sat alone in her cold,

old cottage. Even little, pink Lilly felt lonely. She was the only flower left in the whole village.

Everyone felt agitated and angry. Ugly accusations abounded, but no one could prove anything. And still, no one ever thought to consult The King. Though His arms ached to embrace and comfort them, and though He yearned to share and speak healing words of forgiveness and hope—the people would not come.

By this time, the people hurt deeply, and The King hurt deeply too . . . but for very different reasons. The people hurt deeply because their guilt and shame kept them from looking to the only One who could help them. And The King hurt because in His deep love and profound wisdom, He longed to rescue and restore His beloved people. But they would not turn to Him.

More time came and went. Additional time passed. And yet even more—each day producing its own added distresses and despair. Unrest and uncertainty, selfishness and suspicion suffocated the struggling, little village until the people could stand it no more!

Constable Goforth cried out, ordering the alarm. "Ring the chapel bell! Rally all the people! Gather them together! We must decide what to do!" The bell tolled loud and clear in the midst of the dim, cold, dryness and soon everyone was assembled. The once massive, village oaks were now shriveled, ugly stumps, the once vibrant, abundant flowers were now brittle brown dust, and the once thriving square was now filled with a sea of frustrated voices all demanding to be heard at once.

"What's going on here?" yelled Mr. Sharp.

"This is all *your* fault!" shouted Mrs. Tidings.

"Here, here, let's all try to calm down and sort this out," suggested Mayor Hopewell.

"Who's responsible for all this anyway?" retorted Mr. Crafty.

"The Constable better *do* somethin' *fast* or we'll throw *him* in jail!" taunted Mr. Simpleton.

"Ohhh . . . what are we going to *do?*" whispered old Miss Everdear.

They all wanted an answer. They all needed an answer. But nobody had an answer for all that was happening to the broken, dying village of Highland . . . except The King Himself.

Chapter 9

The Beginning Search

His Gifts of Seeking and Yearning

*I*n the middle of the noisy, commotion-filled square stood Colt, quietly tuning out the confusion and chaos around him. He was older now, nearly grown, wiser, and more aware. He'd always been easy-going and well liked, with his quiet smile and heart to help. And He often spent free time with Will and Able, strong friends, good friends, exploring and hiking in the outdoors they all loved so well.

But Colt also needed to take long walks alone in the quiet woods to think. He was on his own in more ways than one, and he knew that only too well. He thought of his ma's long sickness and then death many years before. He thought of his father, wounded and angry, burying his heart and his life in his work—totally absorbed in training The King's horses and, as a result, ignoring his only son. No time for talking. No time for grieving. No time for loving. Colt tried to bridge the chasm between them many times, but his father's silent, relentless indifference over the years had created a wall between them and, at times, Colt could not shake the resentment and pain. Which was why he needed a secret spot to call his own.

Faithful Falls, for which the neighboring village was named, is a very high and narrow falls, with cascading droplets that float on the breeze before billowing into cloudy, white mistiness below. A large, flat rock, about midway up, just to the right of the falls, was perfect for sitting and thinking, and he welcomed the occasional, refreshing spray that enveloped him there. Colt had found the spot quite by accident while climbing that steep and dangerous side. The rock was cool and secluded, hidden by low-hanging tree boughs. Colt had never even told Will and Able about it. He called it Contemplation Cove, a secret place where he could think more freely and evaluate life more clearly.

Colt sometimes thought of the rock's location, realizing that in life itself, he could climb higher or retreat lower in any decision or action in his life. His thoughts often turned to The King and their perfect times together, of their climb up Mt. Triumph, and of The King's great goodness. But the joy was always short-lived as the pain of the present again permeated his mind and heart. He missed The King. He longed for The King's presence in his life . . . and he knew it.

Now, as the noisy village once again intruded upon his thoughts, Colt felt pressured, surrounded by all the angry people, shouting and complaining, even bumping and stumbling into him. But he stood there . . . rock-solid . . . firm and sure . . . alone . . . in the midst of the clamoring crowd. He sensed a deep, inner need, an inexpressible yearning, a distinct drawing to look toward the hazy grayness to the east. He searched and searched until finally, he detected the indistinct, barely visible, yet shining castle beyond.

Sage and Serena, carrying their two small children, Charity and Scout, walked forward and joined Colt. Sage looked directly at Colt and a nod of acknowledgment and commitment connected them instantly. Sage not only built chapels and barns and fences, he also sought to build up people and they loved him for it. And the people always noticed that, when he headed home to Serena each evening after work, he stopped here or there to search for a sparkling little stone or some other secret token of his love for her. And once home, he faithfully placed it in a secret drawer he had built just for her in her favorite nightstand. And each night she found the gift . . . and smiled.

Sage also loved to find secret spots to play Hide-n-Go-Seek with little Charity and Scout. Other times he would help them carry fishing poles to fishing holes at dawn, or coach them where to spy for fireflies at dusk. On very special evenings, Sage would carry them off to bed and tell them amazing stories about The King and of the glory of the *Dream Days*. He told them of The King's love and wisdom, and Charity and Scout always begged him to tell them more. But he tucked them in snugly and whispered, "Until next time." Then he kissed them on the nose and blew out the candle. But as he headed down the stairs, he would remember more of the former times . . . and there was no quick smile. There was no twinkle in his eyes. And all that was left of the little smudge upon his cheek . . . was a smear.

Back in the noisy, crowded square, Sage and his family stood with Colt in the tiny circle they were forming in the square. Together they gazed toward the distant, yet glowing and towering fortress of The King.

Joy and Gracie were almost grown now too, and also more perceptive and attentive. Joy had a sparkle that everyone loved. Even critical Mr. Sharp melted and relinquished a slight smile whenever he saw her. Gracie quietly won the hearts of the villagers each time she helped a small child, or sat with anxious old Miss Everdear, or volunteered at one of the shops. Most never knew of all her kindnesses behind the scenes, but Joy managed to find out about many of them and that endeared Gracie to her all the more.

Back in the square, both noticed Colt's initiative and intently searching eyes. They noticed Sage's family, too, and quietly came up to Colt and stood, one on either side of him, and their eyes began to pierce the cloudiness, too, drawn to the distant radiance and beauty of The King's castle.

Next came Mr. Hunter Goforth, the Constable, and his wife, Constance, the schoolteacher. They moved into the small circle and looked eastward as well. As the Constable, he was always available to help, but he had a sternness about him that defied small talk and pleasantries. He was strong and serious, always concerned, first and foremost, with the safety of the people.

As the village schoolteacher, Mrs. Goforth was, in contrast, particularly warm and caring, always concerned with the welfare of the children, whether in school or out. She had noticed that Chase, a quick-eyed boy, often got into trouble at the square, stealing produce and running from the shopkeepers. They would always run after Chase, but eventually gave up because he was just too fast for them. And, of course, he ate the evidence.

One day when Chase threw a stone on a dare, breaking one of the chapel windows, Mrs. Goforth didn't scold him. She saw her opportunity and just told him matter-of-factly, "Well, Chase, I'll look forward to your company after school each day this month. You can help me clean the school room, the chalk boards, the pot-bellied stove . . . and the outhouse."

And that's exactly what Chase did. A few times he tried to sneak out the back door when Mrs. Goforth wasn't looking, but Constable Goforth was waiting for him, pointing him right back inside until he finished the work and paid for the stained glass window pane. During their times together after class, Mrs. Goforth showed a regard and respect for Chase's hard work that he never forgot.

Mrs. Goforth was attentive to all the other children, too. She had intentionally seated quiet Gracie right next to outgoing Joy their very first day of school. And sure enough, the girls had become best friends from that moment on.

Next into the growing circle came Gramma and Grampa Hart. That's what everyone called the gentlest, oldest couple in the village. They always had a batch of warm sugar cookies or a handful of fresh blueberries whenever children like little Charity and Scout came to visit. And the Harts always had a happy story to tell in the marketplace or a small coin to share in the square when someone was in need. Now, back in the square with Colt and Sage and the others, Gramma and Grampa Hart held cold, aged hands and stood with them, peering over spectacles toward the distant, gleaming castle beyond.

And then . . . there was Shy. She stayed a safe distance away from the crowd, watching alone, by a bent, old, oak. She was a plain, thoughtful girl with soft eyes, about Joy and Gracie's age. She saw the group forming, but kept an isolated distance. She realized what they were trying to do and sought to catch a glimpse of the castle as well. She longed to be with them, but hesitated. She always hesitated. She didn't know why. And so she remained alone.

One by one, the other villagers saw the little group forming, slowly quieted down, and stopped to gaze through the cloudy haze. The distant castle beyond was truly magnificent in its form, beauty, and glory. And suddenly a great revelation seized them:

> We have to go to The King.
> We need to go to The King.
> We want to go to The King!

As thoughts turned to words and then to plans to see if He would meet with them, frail Gramma and Grampa Hart tried to clarify a dim remembrance, a fleeting memory, an elusive thought that seemed to whisper within them. They sought to unlock some forgotten door, to grasp some hidden clue, to remember some faded memory of The King and of something very, very good . . . but they could not quite recall what it was.

Chapter 10

The Humble Journey

His Gifts of Invitation, Welcome . . . and Hope

Colt looked resolutely through the dimness to the radiant castle of The King, far, far away. Then without turning to the right or to the left, he took the first deliberate step forward. Many of the other villagers followed him, resolving to begin their journey east to see The King. They thought of all the times The King had called to them, written to them, visited them, and greeted them openly. Yet in return, they had ignored His words, refused His kindnesses, and rejected His presence. Heavy thoughts weighed on their hearts and silenced them.

The older ones remembered the past and the choices they had made, while the younger ones had pieced together different parts of the story that had been mentioned here and there over the years. Everyone knew enough to ask themselves, *"Why did I treat Him that way? Why have I been so unkind? Why did I think He was to blame?"*

Sage and Serena, carrying little Charity and Scout, helped lead the trek, too, encouraging children as well as adults along the way, making sure everyone had warm coats, hats, and scarves. They watched as identical little triplets, Faith, Hope, and Love, all with long brown hair and identical freckles sprinkled across their cheeks, held hands very, very tightly, and huddled together as they gently stepped forward. Old Miss Everdear followed, pulling her little pink coat closer, clutching her little pink satchel, and looking up to check on little pink Lilly who shivered in the silence. Serena noticed old Miss Everdear and held out an extra pink scarf, which she gratefully accepted.

But some stayed behind—like Mr. Sharp and Mr. Crafty. They seethed with bitterness and anger and refused to go. They did not consider The King worth knowing. And they even tried to discourage others with scoffing words and jeering taunts. But the drawn and determined ones slowly started up Pursuer's Pathway, the narrow lane leading to the great and glorious castle of The King.

Chase stayed behind, kicking his feet in the dirt, debating whether to join the crowd or stay back with the tough boys in the village. He'd made it on his own this far. He could handle himself. He'd even held his own against the biggest, meanest boy, a bully and a thief named Robb. The other boys had witnessed that and didn't bother Chase anymore.

Still, he didn't have any real friends. He felt empty, like something was missing from his life. He realized he was restless . . . and lonely. He took a hesitant step forward toward the lane, then quickly glanced around to see if anyone had noticed him. His mind tempted him to stay behind. But his heart urged him to step forward. At the very last possible moment ... he darted up the lane toward the others.

Shy had been watching him from the shadows. She hesitated too. She saw that the crowd was almost out of sight now, and she wanted to join them. She didn't want to be left behind. She finally took one step, and then another. She slowly crept forward and managed to keep the crowd in sight. Eventually she reached the outskirts of the group. No one noticed her. She felt invisible and unimportant. She felt like she blended in everywhere and fit in nowhere.

Shy plodded along, pulling her old gray coat closer. Her thoughts wandered back to all the times Joy and Gracie had invited her to join them for games at recess, or to share lunches at school, or to walk home together. But Shy had always nodded a slow no and turned away. She'd wanted to say yes but something had held her back. Joy and Gracie never thought Shy was rude or unkind when she refused. They just sensed that she seemed sad or hurt somehow.

Shy straggled and struggled along, still at the back of the crowd. She felt alone, unworthy, and unwanted. A constant pain deep in her heart pressured and bullied her. It had been there for as long as she could remember. Sometimes she felt like the intense pain in her heart would burst within her . . . but it never did.

The rest of the crowd trudged along, too, pondering all that had happened. It had been a trying time back at the village and now it was a sad, slow journey, yet they kept moving on. As they slowly rounded a bend, they were startled as a brilliant, massive entrance called Golden Gates gracefully swung open wide to welcome them. The stately gateway was dazzling despite the sun's absence, with a radiance all its own. And the gates seemed to gently beckon the seeking travelers to come, all who are weak and weary and weighed down.

The people gratefully continued forward toward the towering, elegant entry, realizing they were entering The King's vast, official lands. Will and Able raced through the crowd and reached the gates first—but suddenly stopped. All the others slowed to a confused and silent halt too. Both young men stood very still, one on either side of the gates, for a long moment. They stared at each other—as if daring the other to go first. Colt, near the front of the crowd, turned slightly, caught their attention, and hinted that he just might go through first. That broke the tension. Will and Able suddenly laughed and bolted through the gates together! All the others breathed a sigh of relief as they gratefully began to pass through, too. And they noticed that the castle was a bit clearer and a bit nearer, too.

As the dim lane encouraged them along, Sage reached for Serena's hand, and noticing how cold it was, gently warmed it in his own. His thoughts wandered to the day The King had brought all those men from Faithful Falls to help him complete the village chapel, the biggest and best job he'd ever done. He thought of the countless other kindnesses The King had shared with him as well, and the pain within his heart grew heavier. Serena felt it, too.

Charity and Scout walked beside their parents, quiet and confused. They didn't understand all that was going on but they were very tired. Charity whispered to her little brother, "I just wish we could go back and get some more warm, sugar cookies from Gramma Hart," and Scout quickly bobbed his head up and down in agreement, wishing he could race her there right now.

Old Miss Everdear was worn and weary, too. As she continued to walk along the dusty, dim pathway, she was still able to catch glimpses, here and there, of exquisite, marble sculptures in The King's vast lands and lovely gardens. One statue was of a tall, robed shepherd, radiating light from within and gently holding a small lamb, with several others by his side. The stately figure was called . . . The Lover of the Lambs.

It reminded old Miss Everdear of her visits with The King and of the comfort and love she had always felt in His presence. She stopped for a moment and then stepped forward, reaching out to touch the gentle figure. But a sudden wave of intense sadness so overwhelmed her . . . she slowly withdrew her hand. Even little, pink Lilly lay limp and lifeless and languishing. Old Mayor Hopewell was the only one who noticed Miss Everdear. He quietly came alongside her, offering his arm for support. She looked into his gentle eyes and gratefully accepted.

As the two walked on together along the dreary pathway, old Miss Everdear also caught a brief glimpse of a lovely water feature framed by gentle, lush green willows and called Overflowing Fountain. A central burst of water, glowing with light, soared into the air, then splashed gently into a large, alabaster basin directly below, before spilling over onto the surrounding terraces. The water flowed gently from tier to tier upon glistening, white rock formations and around clusters of crimson and white blossoms before swirling into sparkling pools. It was breathtaking in its beauty and stunning in its shimmering purity. It gave old Miss Everdear some much-needed encouragement . . . and hope. Serena felt the same and they exchanged grateful glances.

As the people walked further along, they noticed that the lane had definitely become steeper and harder to climb. Suddenly, a few of the villagers stopped in the middle of the pathway, refusing to go one step further. Mrs. Sharp was one and she snarled at them all. "I'm not going any farther. I can't stand the thought of groveling before that King. You're all cowards. I'm going back and if you had any pride left, you'd join me!" and with that, she whirled around and started back against the tide of people, shoving aside whoever stood in her way.

Mr. Simpleton spoke next. "This journey isn't worth it. It's totally unnecessary and there's no point to it! I'd be a fool to keep going. I'm heading back to Highland and if you're smart, you'll come with me!" And with that, he called out, "Mrs. Sharp . . . oh, Mrs. Sharp . . . !" and hurried after her.

At that point, Smithy Armstrong stopped. And when he stopped, they all stopped. He had a blank look, and drops of sweat trickled down his face despite the cold. The people looked at him with concern and confusion, wondering what was wrong.

Smithy stared at them, searching each face with weary, disheartened eyes, and finally said, "I - I can't do this anymore. It isn't worth it. I've struggled and plodded along this path and for what? There's nothing here. I'm going back to make a life for myself and my family. The King doesn't care about me. He doesn't care about you. Let's go back and start again. We're strong. We can make this work together. We can do this on our own." And as he turned and started back, everyone turned and watched as the burly giant gently walked through the crowd coaxing others to join him.

Everyone was stunned. No one could move. Everyone's resolve was shaken. How could Smithy Armstrong . . . of all people . . . give up? He was the strongest man in the community. He had helped build the new chapel. He had helped build the new well. Everyone knew and loved Smithy. Awkward, silent moments slowly ticked by as everyone thought about Smithy's disheartened retreat.

Colt eventually looked over at Sage and they both knew what they would do. Together, they both turned back around and looked straight ahead. First Colt, and then Sage and Serena, Constable and Mrs. Goforth, even fragile Miss Everdear—and Chase of all people—slowly and deliberately stepped forward. And as they did so, others chose to move forward too.

Mr. and Mrs. Leary silently watched as Gramma and Grampa Hart took weak, faltering steps forward. They nodded to each other and came alongside to help the elderly couple. Little Scout, restless and tired, carelessly flung a few stones, but with one glance from his papa, he quietly dropped the last few pebbles by the side of the path. And the Goforths noticed that tiny Faith, Hope, and Love were stumbling along, cold and frightened. They gently gathered them into their arms and carried them on.

Time seemed to drag on endlessly. They hoped that The King would see them. And they hoped that He would help them. And they hoped that it was not too late . . . for they all realized now . . . that He was the only hope they had.

Chapter 11

The Highest Truth

His Gifts of Free Forgiveness and Real Relationship

The villagers persisted on their journey, eventually rounding a long, gentle curve to the right. Suddenly everyone gasped! Just ahead, a sweeping vista opened up, revealing a vast expanse of immense mountains and graceful river valleys. The sheer enormity of it all combined with the sense of profound peace and unmistakable power awed them. And central to the captivating beauty, atop the rising hill before them, stood The Magnificent Castle of The Great King of Glory!

Light and brilliance streamed forth from every window. Vibrance and strength emanated from its massive arches and stately spires . . . and wisps of pure, white clouds floated amidst its twelve pointed parapets and chiseled towers. A faint melody drifted out to them and the soothing fragrance of frankincense warmly invited them on.

All eyes soon rose to the top balcony where they could clearly distinguish The King Himself, their handsome, strong, and gracious King of Glory, waving a warm and lively welcome! He looked as though He had been waiting a long, long, time just for them . . . and He had! He appeared to be incredibly happy and excited to see them coming . . . and He was! He seemed to have an amazing smile that each and every person somehow sensed was intended just for them . . . and it was!

Suddenly, all the villagers started surging forward. They had seen their King! And He was welcoming them! "Come on!" shouted Sage as he encouraged everyone onward. Many started jogging. Others began skipping. And soon everyone was racing.

"Faster!" cried Constable Goforth. Up the winding pathway they all came pouring! Through the spacious fields they all came rushing! Over the sloping meadows they all came streaming! Drawing nearer and nearer to their King, they were running and jumping and dancing. They were laughing and leaping and bursting with joy! But they steadfastly kept their eyes on their King, as He steadfastly kept His loving eyes on them, every step of their way back to Him. They saw Him as He stood there on the balcony, the tall, regal, powerful King of Glory, His royal robes billowing in the breeze, radiance shining from His very being, and arms open wide in welcome!

Joy and Gracie smiled warmly at The King, and The King smiled back with pure pleasure! Sage lifted Charity and Scout onto his broad shoulders just as the crowd swept them forward, and The King grinned with sheer delight. And even old Miss Everdear merrily broke into a hobbily, wobbily jog, as little pink Lilly jiggled and giggled with joy! And The Mighty King threw back His mighty head and laughed aloud with a mighty joy!

Suddenly—without warning—the celebrating throng instantly came to a shocking and terrible halt—unable to move forward! They faltered and floundered and fell to their knees with a thunderous pounding that shook the very ground, and hollow echoes of their fall rumbled and then faded into the empty valleys beyond. Men, women, and children knelt in despair, sensing an invisible invincible veil of some kind, separating them from their Great and Glorious King. Their minds turned to the contamination of sin deep within. They grieved over the wrongs they had committed. And they mourned the indescribable anguish that had destroyed their lives with The King and with one another.

Everyone that is—except Mr. Leary. He stood at the back of the crowd, his heart recoiling at the concept of conviction. He feared the shame and guilt that plagued him, but yet cringed at the thought of confessing. Slowly he took a step back, and then another. He backed away from his wife . . . from The King . . . and from that place. Mrs. Leary turned and their eyes met. She saw the tormenting doubt and yet the deliberate refusal in his stare. She called to him but he turned away, blocking her pleadings from his mind, and stumbling blindly back down the path. She watched him, unwilling to move from her place. She called to him yet again, but he was soon out of sight. It was then that there escaped from her a grief-stricken, gut-wrenching cry that pierced the silence and the heart of every person present.

They all began to mourn their choices and lives. How could their evil hearts ever dare whisper the words *pardon* or *forgiveness* or *grace*? How could they ever speak such words before the most honorable and just King of all kings? They had chosen to steal the gift. They had caused their broken relationships and their broken spirits. They had chosen lives of selfishness. And most horrific of all, they had committed the vilest, most wretched act of all. They had willfully killed The King's dear, innocent, beloved, and only Son. The tragic darkness of it all vividly assaulted their minds and crushed their hearts.

They bowed their heads as sobs of sorrow wrenched their bodies and thoughts of death racked their minds. Many wept aloud uncontrollably. Others were strangely silent, unable to give voice to the grief that engulfed them.

But the commanding voice of The Great King pierced through the darkness of that moment as He called out to each and every heart, "Look up! See the salvation of your King!" And as each head rose, each soul gasped! There on the balcony with The King stood . . . THE SON! The Son of The King of Glory! He was . . . ALIVE! And He stood there before them in equal power and majesty with The King. Flashes of lightning pierced the sky as great rolls of thunder cracked and echoed throughout the realm. Billowing winds gusted and swirled as The Powerful King and The Mighty Son stood together in all their glory before the great throng of people.

Oh, the deep, deep mystery of this great King of all kings as He called out to them all! "I reign with absolute Justice and I accurately declare the truth of your sentence of death for your wrongs. But I also equally declare the truth of My great Mercy, by accepting the death of My innocent Son in your place, as payment for your wrongs . . . if you will believe Me. My Son gave His life . . . to give *you* life . . . for that is how much I value and treasure you!" And then, this unstoppable King with His triumphant resurrection power declared, "I have brought My Son back from the vice-grip of death into the realm of the living, proving once and for all: I alone have the authority and power to decide right and wrong. I alone have the authority and power to decide life and death. And I alone have the authority, power, and grace to provide true life.

> "'The Highest Truth' is that
> I forgive and I restore relationship
> . . . forever . . . to whoever will ask Me."

And there The Great King of Glory stood on His balcony, with His heart and arms still open wide in welcome, still offering forgiveness and grace, love and relationship to all who would ask. Each and every person there bowed their head solemnly in personal prayer, admitting and confessing their wrongs. They humbly accepted The King's offer of The Son's sacrifice. And they humbly acknowledged The Son's death in their place . . . as payment for *their* death penalty. The King looked upon them all in that holy moment and declared, "My dear ones, I forgive you. Your sins are gone now and forevermore, and we are united eternally!" There, they believed The King. There, they trusted His Words. There, they experienced the truth of His loving, forgiving, amazing Grace. And there, they experienced the indescribable transfer through The Invisible Veil, as the incredible supernatural power of The King drew and elevated them into His eternal spiritual realm, out of the clutches of the kingdom of darkness, and into His Glorious Kingdom of Light!

The King called out with great joy for all to hear, "It is impossible for unbelievers to penetrate The Invisible Veil. But you have chosen to believe, and belief has enabled you to transcend it! You are officially and forevermore in My beautiful, spiritual Kingdom and a member of My eternal, spiritual family! Nothing can ever separate us again!"

Then The King shared a final, very important thought. "You will still live temporarily in this physical world for a time as we live life together . . . but My spiritual kingdom is now and forever within you! It is not heaven. Heaven will come later. But with all its glorious light and beauty, do you think it is, perhaps, just a little glimpse of the heavenly realms you will one day know and enjoy forevermore?" And the people erupted into cheers of rejoicing that knew no bounds and grateful hearts that burst with ethereal joy!

Chapter 12

The Spiritual Celebration!

His Gifts of Victory, Freedom, and Peace

Everyone started talking and reconciling and celebrating The King's grace altogether! Joy and Gracie turned to each other, remembering how they had made each other jealous years ago and, at the same moment, both said, "I'm sorry," and hugged. Sage found Miss Everdear in the crowd and humbly apologized for charging her extra for the tree and they hugged, too. And Mrs. Tidings walked over to Colt and gently reached out to touch his cheek. Colt was taller than she was now and smiled down at her. They both remembered what had happened, but the pain was gone now for both of them. Colt touched her cheek . . . and then suddenly reached down and lifted the pleasingly plump little lady right off her feet with joyful abandon and twirled her around till her jolly laugh filled the air here, there, and everywhere! It was definitely a day of celebration for all!

Charity remembered stealing a sweet roll and went over and told Mr. Baker how sorry she was. Chase walked over to Will and Able and mumbled an apology—for bullying them one day in the woods—something no one else knew about except those three. Will and Able accepted Chase's words and then Will said, "Okay . . . but that means we have to be friends now!" Chase looked up in surprise . . . and then smiled. Able chimed in with, "By the way, it sure took you long enough to decide to start this journey!" Chase was shocked! They had seen his uncertainty and doubts after all! And yet somehow . . . it just didn't matter anymore. Old things were indeed past. The new had come!

The dark, cold, deadness that had plagued the people for so long had disappeared, and the brilliant, warm sunshine reappeared, streaming forth in all its light and life revealing all the beauty all around them! Everyone was rejoicing when, suddenly, their regal King—the commanding King of Glory—did something absolutely amazing! He reached out and grasped the balcony railing with His powerful hands, flung Himself over the ornate bannister, catapulted His mighty frame to the landscaped grounds seven stories below—and with robe flowing and heart glowing—He started running toward His beloved people, to embrace them one and all! Astounded, they all looked at each other! And then with sheer joy and abandon, they started racing toward Him, too . . . casting off heavy coats, flinging hats high into the clear, clean air, and scattering mittens and scarves absolutely everywhere!

It was magnificent beyond all measure to tell!
It was wondrous beyond all words to convey!
It was awesome beyond all comprehension
to express!

The children were laughing! The women were crying with joy! And the men were competing to reach The King first! The people were dashing toward their King! And their King was racing toward His beloved people!

It was joy!
It was rapture!
It was bedlam!

Dogs were barking! Birds were singing! Children were squealing! And the men and women were cheering for sheer joy! The King—with The Son suddenly by His side—reached Their people, and everyone surrounded Them with hugs and laughter and super-abounding joy! And every single person there—absolutely every single one—got to hug The Magnificent King of Glory and The Majestic Son Himself! . . . Even Shy? Even Shy.

The King swung children high into the sweet-scented air, and then He placed others on His broad, cozy lap to rest for a while. Some wanted to touch His hair or His robe or His face. Others just wanted to gaze into His deep, gentle eyes and soak in His love for a long, long time. Mothers wanted to touch His strong hands, and fathers wanted to rest their hands on His powerful shoulders. All felt welcome. Everyone came near. And everybody basked in the overwhelming love of their amazing King.

Eventually, a very old woman, stooped and bent low, slowly made her way toward The King, and the crowd, as they gradually became aware, parted to make way for her. She had a very visible scar . . . under her left eye. A very old man, stooped and bent low, slowly made his way to her side, held her hand, and together moved toward The King. He had a very visible scar . . . by his left temple. They hesitated, even stopping once or twice to look into each other's eyes as tears of pain rolled down their cheeks. But they feebly continued forward. It was Gramma and Grampa Hart. It was Gramma . . . Victoria Hart and Grampa Victor Hart—the two who had stolen the gift so many years ago!

They were so weak and aged now—far beyond their years—by deep grief and crushing guilt, that each step they took was painfully awkward and slow. Sage and Serena quietly came alongside and gently helped them on their way. The King saw them coming, their faces down, trudging toward Him—their hearts still feeling a desperately heavy weight that had already been lifted.

The King moved slowly toward the couple as the couple slowly moved toward Him. The people stood breathless as He continued to walk graciously forward. Victor and Victoria reached The King and stood downcast before Him. Without a word, The King tenderly lifted their faces up and met their eyes with such radiance and acceptance and grace, that the weight on their hearts suddenly fell away—gone forevermore! The King gently enfolded them, drawing them to His heart, with all the love the universe could hold. The ladies were all crying. The men were all laughing so they wouldn't cry! And Victor and Victoria felt a peace they had not experienced for many, many years!

And at The King's miraculous touch, forgotten memories flooded their minds with marvelous remembrances of Him from long ago, of cool walks in the abundant gardens, of loving conversations by the sparkling waterfalls, and of starlit joys on the mountaintops. They realized and understood that He truly had been their help in ages past and was now and forevermore their joy and peace to come.

Suddenly, Serena exclaimed, "Look!" and the people turned to behold the sight. Everywhere, as the warm sun continued streaming down on every happy head and heart, and all was light and life and beauty, brand new buds started budding and fragrant new flowers started flowering. Beautiful new blossoms started blossoming and towering new trees started treeing—right before their very eyes! Yes! Yes! If buds can bud and flowers can flower and blossoms can blossom, then trees can tree! At least in Glory they can!

The happy people rejoiced at the breathtaking beauty and then gradually began to sit down in small groups to rest from their long, hard journey and amazing transformation. They relaxed on the lush green lawns in front of the castle and under the shady oaks that were clustered around the grounds. And one oak hid Scout, who was happily climbing higher and higher—hoping to reach the very top so he could wave to The King!

Caring Christina and Gentle Gloria relaxed on the soft grass on their backs, looking up as the cloud formations changed from butterflies to angels to castles in the air. And they marveled at the gentle beauty . . . that is, until Purity suddenly nibbled and tickled their ears!

Other children hummed and played in the warm, renewing sunlight as birds sang sweetly in the trees and as the fragrance of jasmine and violets lingered lightly over them all. Then The Son called out, "Victory!" and a huge, majestic deer—a bold and powerful buck—walked gracefully from the south woods to a clearing near them all. He bowed one knee low, and waited patiently while The Son gently lifted little Charity and Scout onto his back. Together they held on tightly as Victory turned and bounded up and over the hills, springing and half flying on an exhilarating adventure ride. They felt his strong muscles propelling them forward, the fresh wind on their faces, and the thrill of sheer abandon deep in their hearts! Oh, the victory . . . of victory!

Then The Son called out, "Freedom!" and a huge, soaring eagle glided down and landed regally on the castle steps. The Son nodded and Colt was the first to climb upon its large, powerful wings, and soon they were rising high over the castle's towers with breathtaking swiftness. Colt felt the exhilaration of speed and power and height, and his heart raced as they soared through the clear blue skies. Then together, they drifted motionlessly in mid-air, floating between heaven and earth, as Colt experienced the breathless wonder of it all. Then, slowly and gracefully, they circled the castle and descended to a regal landing back upon the castle steps. Oh, the freedom . . . of freedom!

Then The Son called out, "Peaceful!" and a stunningly magnificent swan floated to the northern shore of Delightful Waters, a lovely lake by the front lawns to the right of the castle. The northern shore sparkled as if diamonds lay on its still surface while the southern shore's fountains periodically burst forth with soaring spurts, splashing down upon the happy, squealing children playing there.

The Son offered old Miss Everdear His hand and gently helped her as she nestled onto Peaceful's soft, comfortable feathers. He joined her and they floated and talked of all that had happened and all that was new forevermore. She relaxed in His presence and dipped her hand into the refreshing waters while little pink Lilly basked in the warming sunshine. Then Lilly leisurely leaned over the little, ruffled rim of Miss Everdear's little cap . . . and suddenly winked at her! Old Miss Everdear laughed with surprise and delight and The Son joined in too! Oh, the peace . . . of peace.

Eventually dinnertime drew near, and The King's massive and abundant banquet table was set near the water's edge under a sheer veil with sparkling, clear lights. Musicians came out, playing on wind chimes and strings and soft lutes. Bakers brought out golden trays of lovely, sumptuous delicacies, sugared sweets, and exotic, spiced dishes for all to enjoy. And the Tastemaster shared his vast array of flavorful nectars, multi-colored teas, and sparkling waters truly fit for The King and His people.

And one server, with both hands balanced precariously over his head, held a platter that was bigger than he was! And on it was the biggest and best, most flavorful, braided loaf of golden bread anyone had ever seen or tasted in their entire lives.

The King basked in the presence of His beloved people. Children took turns sitting with Him and sharing stories or whispering secrets that no one else knew. Charity, with eyes sparkling, told The King about one of her scary adventures. "When I was very little, I stumbled and fell into the pond, and my papa reached out and scooped me right up in his fishing net!" Everyone laughed, imagining the sight, and then she added, "And Scout was so happy and hugged me so hard, he practically squeezed me dry!" The people, captivated by her endearing story, laughed with sheer delight!

Those in the middle of their youth told The King jokes and funny experiences. Jovial shared, "I lost my balance in our barn's hayloft last fall. It's really high up there, and so I bounced and bounced from bale to bale all the way down till I landed perfectly on our horse, Grazer, in his stall! It was incredible I didn't break my neck! In fact, it looked as if I'd planned the whole thing . . . like I was just getting ready to go horseback riding for the afternoon!" The boys all hooted and the girls all giggled. Mothers and fathers sat close by too, listening or joining in here and there, and yet still marveling . . . to be in the presence of The Awesome and Amazingly Great King of Glory.

Chapter 13

The Deepest Truth

His Gifts of a New Spirit and The Son Within

*F*orgiveness and grace, restoration and joy, filled the day to overflowing. But eventually, one by one, the people quieted down and met each other's glances as the unanswered questions started to form in their minds, from the oldest to the youngest.

Why had the sun stopped shining back in the village?
And what does living in The King's grace mean?
And most of all . . . what does living in grace
look like day by day?

Thoughts and questions moved from one to all, and they became quiet and expectant as everyone turned their minds and eyes to The King. The King saw the faces and hearts of His people, and though they said not a word, He knew that the time had come for Him to share.

The King called out in a strong yet gentle voice, "My precious people, gather 'round and come let us reason together. I will answer the questions that are on your minds and in your hearts." His inviting arms motioned them all forward, and the people gathered about Him. He sat upon a large flat boulder called Revelation Rock, right by the western edge of Delightful Waters. His Son sat at His right side, and The King waited patiently for each and every one, from the oldest to the youngest, to find a place around Him, and each and every one found a place. Even Shy? . . . Even Shy.

As The King began to share, a warm breeze rustled His long, royal robes, catching wisps of His hair. Strength and goodness emanated from His being, and His countenance glowed with such radiance that they were in awe of Him. "My dearest people," He began, "so near and dear to my heart, I have longed to experience just this moment with you, to pour out My love upon you, and to share the deepest truths of life with you. Now this time has truly come." And for a precious moment in time, all was peaceful and still as they waited in His presence.

Then The King began with the truths of the past: of their perfect relationship, of the temptation by the evil stranger, of their doubting The King's great goodness, of their choice to steal the gift, of their destroyed relationships both with Him and with one another, of their spirit being broken beyond repair, and of His relentless attempts to restore relationship. They knew that all He said was true. They also now knew that they had believed a lie—that they were unlovable, unworthy, unacceptable, and unimportant to The King. And He whispered very softly to them,

"A broken spirit . . . breaks your heart."

Everyone solemnly agreed, and The King continued. "Each of you rejected Me to live life on your own, until you learned that you weren't meant to live this life alone." They sensed very keenly His sorrow and then their own, for they had lost, for a long time, all that He had designed for them, all that they were just now beginning to understand and experience: the Victory of Truth, the Freedom of Forgiveness, the Power of Peace . . . and the all-encompassing Love of The King. The people were eager now to receive His next words to guide them for they truly wanted to understand His will and ways.

The wise King explained, "We were separated, our relationship broken forever—unless I intervened. And the dying sunlight was the result.

My heart's desire was to set you free from the
darkness and lies that were hurting you.
I did it to encourage you to seek a truth
far greater than My gifts.
I did it to encourage you to seek
the greatest Gift of all."
He paused for a long moment and whispered,
"I did it to encourage you to search . . . for Me."

Everyone was stunned and speechless. Such treasures of truth astounded them! The King spoke further. "You already received My first gift, 'The Highest Truth,' when you accepted the grace, forgiveness, and restored relationship I offered to you earlier today from the balcony. You are forgiven once, for all things. My Son died once to pay for all your wrongs . . . past, present, and future. It is finished."

Then The King stood and continued, "That gift was provided at infinite price by My dear Son, and it is precious beyond all measure indeed." He turned to His beloved Son and motioned for Him to stand as well. It appeared as though His mighty heart just might burst with love and pride as He hugged His Son with a oneness of Spirit absolutely beautiful to behold!

Then The King turned to the people and said, "Do you realize that I love you as much as I love My dear Son? I want you to know that I alone decide your value and your worth, and you are far more precious than gold and diamonds and rubies. I declare this now and forever! Some people may build you up and others may tear you down. Neither determines your true worth and value. I do. And I gave My Son's life for you. You are treasured by Me forever. Be at peace." The people were quiet, stunned and speechless, trying to grasp the wonder of His words.

The King spoke in great earnest now. "My greatest desire now is that you believe 'The Deepest Truth' of all and it is this . . . " Here He paused to emphasize His next words with revelation power, and each heart was hushed in holy silence.

"At the moment I forgave you of all of your wrongs and restored our relationship, your old, broken spirit within you *died* and was *taken away* . . . forever! And it was *replaced* with a brand new, beautiful, pure spirit. You are now born again, born anew, born of the spirit. And that is your *new identity*. That is who you truly are now. Even more . . . I have provided for My perfect Son to come and live in your new spirit. And The King repeated His powerful words once more.

"'The Deepest Truth'
is that you are a pure new spirit
and My Son now lives in you."

The King spoke gently now. "You have already believed—by faith—that you have received My forgiveness and restored relationship. Now I ask you to also believe—by faith—that I have given you a pure, new spirit and placed My Son within you. He is not in you merely to *help* you in your *own* efforts to try to be good. Instead, He has already proven His abilities to live this life perfectly, and He asks you to believe that He can live His life *with* you and *in* you and *through* you now. He wants to flow out of your *spirit* and bring victory to your *soul!*

The crowd sat astonished! *Was it really true? Could they stop struggling to earn love? Could they stop striving to gain acceptance? Could they now simply trust and rest in the loving forgiveness and acceptance of The King, and in the inspiring presence and power of The Son within them? With a new spirit, could He truly transform their souls?*

Gramma and Grampa Hart sat side by side in the sunshine, seeking to understand The King's amazing words. Charity and Scout looked quite quizzical trying to grasp such big thoughts. But Chase stole away to the woods nearby . . . full of as much anger as he had ever known in all his life.

There in the shadows Chase scowled, trying to make sense of his sordid life. His parents had had only hardness toward him for as long as he could remember. He'd been thrashed enough times for not finishing a chore or for sassing his ma to know he needed to stay out of sight and out of mind as much as possible.

Before daybreak, Chase would stuff bread and cheese into his pockets and leave before either parent woke up. During the day he'd do his schoolwork just to keep busy, but he'd be ready to fight any boy who back-talked him or talked behind his back. He never went looking for a fight, but he never backed down from one either. And after dark, he'd steal home silently and slip between musty sheets to sleep for a few hours. Over the years, he had hardened himself not to cry, not to feel, and not to care. But sometimes he still did. Why didn't they love him? Why did he feel so worthless? What was wrong with him?

Chase was not only angry, he was confused . . . and not only with his parents. He didn't understand The King either. The King had not stopped his parents' unfair treatment. He had not prevented the pain. Chase admitted he was thankful for the forgiveness The King had offered him, and he felt a peace in his heart now that he'd never known before. But Chase knew The King was now asking him to trust Him in a whole new way, and he was totally unwilling and unable to do so. No one had been there for him growing up, and Chase had no intention of ever being vulnerable and wounded again. No. Never Again. Ever. And he grabbed stones and rocks and whatever else he could find there in the woods, and he threw them as hard as he could, for as long as he could, till his arm ached and his tears stopped.

Chapter 14

The Enlightening Lesson

His Gift of a New Identity

As the people continued to ponder all the deep truths The King had shared, He turned to the Constable and said, "Constable Hunter Goforth." Everyone's eyes turned to the Constable, and he, a bit startled and embarrassed at being singled out from the crowd, stood and said, "Yes, my Lord?" The King smiled kindly to reassure him and then asked, "Hunter, do you remember the day years ago when I gave you your official, authorized Certificate declaring you to be, 'The Honorable Constable of the Lovely Little Village of Highland?'"

"Why . . . yes . . . yes, Sir, I do," Hunter replied. "I remember I was glad to complete the training and honored to be chosen . . . but . . . well, I was uncertain too . . . not quite sure I would be able to do the tasks required."

The King understood and said. "So the truth is, I declared you to be the Constable, but you still didn't think or feel like the Constable yet. You weren't at all sure that you could fulfill the role I had bestowed upon you."

Constable Goforth rubbed the back of his neck uneasily and then said rather sheepishly, "Uh, yes, Sir. That's right." Everyone nodded, sympathizing with him. The King then asked, "Hunter, at what point did you realize that you really are the Constable?"

Constable Goforth thought for a moment and replied, "Well, actually . . . yes . . . it was when I saw those thieves. I was on watch that night, and I spied them crawling over the far south hill toward our village to steal our supplies and destroy our families." The villagers all nodded, remembering that dangerous night.

The Constable continued. "So I galloped through the square and around to all the cottages, raising the alarm, and calling out to everyone to get their guns to defend their homes—and I told them not to shoot unless I gave the order. I remember I raced back through the square to the south gate and hid, waiting for the thieves to approach the entrance. Then I suddenly called out, 'Who goes there?' I caught the thieves off guard, but their leader still threatened us all, calling out, 'Give up right now while you still got time . . . or I'll . . . '

"I interrupted him and shouted right back, loud and clear, for all of them to hear. 'We're ready for you and all your men—and we'll *never* back down! Every window and every door has a gun or a rifle and we will defend our own. Now . . . you get outta here . . . NOW!' When the outlaws saw all the weapons pointed right at them, they backed right down, ran for the hills, and rode away."

Everyone solemnly remembered when Constable Goforth first stood his ground and defended their families and their homes . . . with his life if need be. He had gained the loyalty and love of the whole village that night and from that moment on. The people erupted into cheers of, 'Well done, Hunter!" and "We love you, Constable!" Their ever-serious leader awkwardly glanced down and then, in meticulous succession, straightened his shoulders, jacket, and hat. Everyone understood and smiled, and then turned their attentions back to The King who concluded with, "So Hunter, now you believe and live and act and feel like the Constable of our dear village?"

"Yes," said the Constable clearing his throat. "Yes, Sir, I do."

The King paused, then asked, "So you *were* the Constable before that—but you just didn't quite believe or think or act like one yet?"

"Th-that's true," said The Constable, confused now, but unsure why. The King had another question. "Now Hunter, there have been some times since then when you've made some mistakes . . . say . . . when you hauled Chase in for stealing meat from Mr. Tidings' smokehouse, only to hear Sage confirm that he definitely saw Robb do it." Constable Goforth humbly nodded, acknowledging it was true.

"But," said The King, "even though you made that mistake, you still know and believe that you're the Constable, right?"

"Why . . . yes, yes I do," said Hunter, starting to gain a real understanding now of The King's ultimate point. The King not only wanted him to understand that He had declared him the Constable and His word was true. The King also wanted him to understand that He had also declared him a brand new creation, with a pure, new spirit, and His word was true in this, too. Hunter's heart leapt at such a truth!

Suddenly, his thoughts backtracked to his mistake with Chase, and he turned to the crowd and called out loud and clear, "By the way, believe you me, as soon as I learned the truth about Robb stealing that meat, I sure got Chase out of trouble lickety-split, and I told him I sure was real sorry about accusing him that way!" Laughter rippled through the crowd. They'd all been thinking so hard about The King's questions, that the Constable's sudden and incredibly sincere confession had caught them by surprise! The Constable turned bright red for just an instant. Then he too relaxed and joined in.

As the crowd quieted down, The King concluded with these words. "Hunter, in your new spirit, in your true self, you are now a pure and good man. The occasional mistakes you make on the outside can never change the brand new, pure you on the inside.

"As you grow more and more in understanding this truth and reality on the *inside*, your spirit will transform your soul day by day more and more on the *outside*, where you will be able to see it. Do you believe Me, Hunter?" Constable Goforth nodded gratefully. The King's voice boomed with a regal power and royal authority that shook the very ground.

"I am here today to declare to each of you that you are now a brand new spirit creation . . . good and pure and true. You might not always think or act like one yet, but you are. You may question or doubt it at times, but it's still true. You have been born anew, born of the spirit, born again, pure and good, and your new spirit identity will impact your mind, will, and emotions slowly but surely. The more you believe in My words to you, the more you will rest in My truths for you." A few in the crowd experienced a glimmer of understanding, but many were thoughtful and quiet.

Chapter 15

The Turning Point

His Gifts of Wisdom and Discernment

As the crowd continued to ponder all that The King had shared with them, He turned and saw little Charity perched on her papa's broad shoulders. "Sweet Charity, do you remember being in first grade last year?" Charity was so startled to hear her name mentioned by The King that she almost toppled off her papa's shoulders! But she quickly managed to regain her balance, looked wide-eyed at The Great King of Glory, and managed to nod a silent "Yes."

He smiled very kindly to reassure her and then asked, "Charity, do you also remember at graduation being officially promoted from the first to the second grade?" Charity nodded again.

"And when you walked into your second-grade class this year, did you think and feel like a second-grade student?"

Charity thought back for a moment and shook her head, "N-no, Sir. I didn't. I just felt afraid."

"Did you think you could do second grade work?"

"N-no . . . I didn't."

The King smiled sympathetically, as did all the villagers. Then He continued, "So, when did you know for sure that you were truly a second-grade student?"

Charity thought about it for a moment and then replied, "Well, when Mrs. Goforth said that it was time for all the second-grade students to go out for recess, I just kinda sat there. I wasn't quite sure what to do. The other second graders had gotten up and left so I finally decided to at least try to head for the door. But I watched Mrs. Goforth real careful, you know—to see if she'd tell me to go back and sit down or somethin'. But no, she even looked over at me real kind and said, 'Run along now.' So I decided right then and there, *Okay, I really must be a second-grade student now!* . . . and I never, ever doubted it again!" Laughter filled the air as the crowd enjoyed the scene that Charity had painted for them.

The King then asked, "And are you doing second-grade work now, Charity?"

"Yes, Sir."

"And do you believe . . . and feel . . . and think like a second-grade student now?"

Charity looked right at The King with amazement, and replied, "Why . . . yes, Sir. I do!" and everyone chuckled once more.

The King spoke gently now. "Charity . . . are there times when you make mistakes in your second-grade work?"

Charity nodded a slow, honest, "Yes."

The King continued, "Even then, do you still believe you are really and truly a second-grade student who's learning and growing?"

Charity's eyes lit up with understanding. "Yes . . . yes, Mr. King! I really do!"

The momentum of the moment had arrived as The King announced a second time: "I am here today as the supreme and official authority of this land to declare to each and every one of you that you are now and forevermore—in your spirit—a brand new creation, good and pure and true! You might not think or feel like one yet, but you are. You may question or wonder about it when you make mistakes along the way as you grow but, I assure you, My words to you are true. If you think you are evil on the inside, you will think it natural to do evil. But if you believe My words that you are now truly good on the inside, you will think it natural for you to do good and thus begin to win the battles of life. Knowing your true identity in your spirit with The Son's power within you is the way to ultimate victory!"

The King waited a moment for His words to sink in. Colt wanted desperately to understand. So did Sage and Serena and old Miss Everdear. But it was all so new. It all seemed so hard to understand. The King saw their faces and was ever so patient and kind as He continued to explain their new life.

"When you choose to do something wrong now, because of the stranger's tempting whispers and lies, it simply means you have forgotten who you really are: a pure, good spirit. You have forgotten that you have the power of The Son living within you to overcome any obstacle. You have forgotten that your spirit can totally impact your soul for good. You have forgotten that I meet all your needs for love, security, and purpose, even when others fail you."

Then The King graciously encouraged them. "So when you make a wrong choice now, just come to Me. Yes, admit the wrong, but know that My forgiveness and grace are already yours in abundance. My love and acceptance are rock-solid, and My arms are always open wide to you. The more you believe My truths, the more you will win these battles.

"Be at peace, dear ones.
You bring great joy to My heart,
and I love to love you!"

The people sat amazed at such love and acceptance, such wisdom and truth. Charity, who had been thinking very carefully as The King spoke, very slowly slipped down from her papa's shoulders and looked at The Son. He understood immediately and made His way to her side. Together they held hands and walked forward to stand before The Great King. The crowd stared in silence, waiting to see what would happen.

Charity glanced doubtfully at The Son, but He smiled and reassured her. She was not alone. He was with her. And so, she took a deep breath and began. "M-Mr. King, I was just thinking . . . that . . . well . . . I - I get real mad sometimes when I see the other girls like Joy and Gracie being such best friends and . . . well, I want a best friend . . . and so sometimes I get real jealous and I . . . " She paused here and hung her head. Joy and Gracie glanced at each other, remembering.

Charity was unable to look at The King, but she managed to turn toward Gracie. She gathered her last ounce of courage, and blurted out, "Just a little while ago I got so mad—I knocked Gracie down real hard over by the woods where Victory was giving rides and she cut her leg real bad on a sharp rock and . . . and . . . oh, Mr. King . . . I didn't mean it! I really didn't mean to hurt her! I feel so awful. I'm so very, very sorry."

Tears filled Charity's eyes and spilled onto her checks as she thought of the pain she had caused Gracie, not only on the outside, but on the inside too. Then Charity hesitantly reached down, and gently gathered up Gracie's long skirt just a bit, enough for many of the people nearby to see that the cut was indeed a serious one that needed some cleansing and stitching right away.

Charity slowly met Gracie's eyes. There were as many tears of compassion in Gracie's eyes as there were tears of sorrow in Charity's. The King embraced Gracie and Charity in His powerful arms, and kissed each of them warmly on the cheek. Then The King looked into Charity's eyes and said, "Thank you, Charity, for coming to talk to Me about this. Be assured you are already forgiven, dearly loved, and totally accepted by Me." Charity managed a hesitant, tear-stained smile and then relaxed in His embrace, believing His words.

Then The King looked into Gracie's tearful eyes. "Precious Gracie, you bring so much gentleness to all of us, but you are hurting now, so I will ask Constable Goforth to take you to the castle to help with your wound. But I would first ask, dear one, if you believe in your pure, new spirit that you are truly a forgiver now, and by the power of The Son living within you, that you can honestly and truly forgive Charity for hurting you."

Gracie looked into The King's eyes and gave a knowing smile. Then she turned kindly to Charity and whispered, "I already have." Gracie reached out and squeezed Charity's hand as the crowd witnessed the beautiful exchange. Then the strong Constable came forward, and The King gently placed Gracie into his arms so he could carry her to the castle.

The King picked up Charity, placing her ever so close to His heart, and called out in a voice of authority that commanded everyone's full attention. "I have given everyone free choice. It means that you each choose, moment by moment, whether you will listen to The Son, and live from your pure, new spirit and The Son's power within you, or whether you will listen to the deceptions of the stranger and hurt others as well as yourself. The stranger is your enemy and his desire is to destroy you." And they all saw clearly how true The King's words were and how much damage the stranger had already inflicted on all of them.

The King continued. "Charity, your new spirit, the new you, wants good things for Gracie. Do you remember saying that you didn't mean to hurt her?" Charity realized with new understanding that those were indeed the words of her heart.

The King pressed on. "When you hurt Gracie it was because you were tricked by the enemy. First, he tempted your mind. He planted ideas of worthlessness and rejection, and you *thought* that Gracie was worthy and lovable but you were not. That is a lie. The truth is that you are totally loved and completely accepted by

Me forever." And The King looked into her eyes and smiled.

"Then the enemy tempted your emotions. He introduced loneliness and you *felt* that you were all by yourself, that no one cared, that no one was there for you. That is a lie too. The truth is that The Son is always in you and with you to listen, comfort, and help you."

Charity was trying to grasp The King's words and repeated, "So . . . the enemy tries to get me to think wrong thoughts . . . and to feel wrong feelings?" The King nodded with joy and confirmed her understanding. "That's right, Charity." ...And then He suddenly tickled her little tummy! She squiggled and wiggled and giggled with joy, and laughter rippled through the happy crowd of attentive listeners.

The King then said, "And there was one more way the enemy attacked your soul. He tempted your will—your power to decide. He deceived you into *choosing* to hurt Gracie, to do something wrong, to try to solve your problem. And that is a great lie, too. The truth is that The Son living in you has perfect power to overcome any problems you face. Look to Him, join with Him, and the joy you will experience each time you let His life flow in and through you will be awesome in the highest to behold! Remember:

> "True victory is loving others into their
> own victories in The Son."

What an amazing moment! Charity was learning a great truth that would help her the rest of her life. The enemy would try again to tempt her thoughts and feelings and choices. But she believed that The Son was living in her now, and He could renew her mind, and heal her emotions, and empower her will! Together, they would win the challenges of life that would unfold in the future! She was so excited to learn and lean on Him!

The King then brought the whole lesson to a practical conclusion. "Charity, come and talk with Me more about the best friend you want, knowing I will do what is best for you. There is much to learn about *being* a best friend before having a best friend, and The Son in you will give you all the patience and wisdom you need until that day."

Charity looked into The King's beautiful eyes and then hugged His neck very, very tightly with a heart full of love and hope. Then she slipped down from His arms, waved shyly to Joy nearby, and walked through the supportive crowd back to her waiting family.

Charity was in awe. The King loved her! He loved her and met all her needs for love, security, and purpose. She felt such peace. She knew The King had heard every word of her heart, and He had spoken to her personally and assured her of His truths. She was learning. She thought for a moment and then whispered to her mama and papa that she needed to do something. They watched and then smiled as Charity walked over to Joy . . . and together they headed for the castle door.

Chapter 16

The Living Reality

His Gift of Real Relationship

Chase had heard every word that The King had spoken to Charity. He felt his defenses coming down but fear again desperately kicked in. He had to protect himself. He had to guard against getting too close. He had to keep fighting. He didn't want to let anyone . . . *in*. It hurt too much. And yet he wanted what Charity had.

He vaguely sensed some words trying to reach his mind, words like *Be still* and *I am with you* and *Cast your cares upon Me,* but he couldn't be sure. He saw the love and wisdom of The King guiding Charity, and he wanted that oneness too. Yet when he felt his inner walls collapsing once more, he fought back again. The Son saw Chase struggling and quickly stepped forward for it was time for Him to speak. He called out to each and every villager.

"Good people,
I Am all the love and joy and peace you need,
living in you, filling you first,
and then flowing out of you to others.
I Am your wisdom and truth and righteousness,
living in you, filling you first,
and then spilling out of you onto others.
I Am your grace and power and goodness,
living in you, filling you first,
and then pouring out of you upon others.

Today you have come searching for direction . . .
and I Am the Way.
Today you have come searching for answers . . .
and I Am the Truth.
Today you have come searching
for real relationship . . .
and I Am the Life.
Yes, I Am the Way, the Truth, and the Life *in* you!"

Chase wrestled against each word, resistant and fearful. But Sage and Serena were awed by the wonder of "The Deepest Truth" growing strong and sure within them. And Colt experienced an incredible joy welling up within his heart. Then The Son added:

"I created a perfect world, and though it is now broken, The King and I are here for you. There is still great hope and purpose. Love Me . . . and see your difficult challenges be turned around and used for . . .

a greater good,
a higher purpose,
and a deeper truth,
of freedom and oneness in Me."

And then The Son concluded with His final, all-important words. "You can remain at 'The Highest Truth' with forgiveness assured, but continuing to depend on yourself and outward behavior to measure your value and acceptability as you try to live this life. Or . . . you can go on to 'The Deepest Truth' of all, and believe that you have a pure new spirit and My presence and power within you so we can live this life together." He paused and then asked His final question. "Will you believe Me in this, too?"

Everyone was stunned. No one could speak. No one could move. Did The Son just say that in the midst of this fractured world, their struggles could lead to a greater good? That their difficulties could serve a higher purpose? That their trials could result in a deeper aware-ness of oneness with Him? The profound realization of His words slowly but surely touched their minds and reached their hearts. And suddenly . . . the entire crowd . . . EXPLODED with joy!

Many of the people answered with resounding cries of "I BELIEVE YOU!" People like Colt, Sage and Serena, Charity, Constable and Mrs. Goforth . . . and Chase! He got it! He understood! He knew now! A bright light had suddenly filled his heart and soul with truth and forgiveness and grace! How had The Son said it? He was the love and goodness and peace Chase yearned for. He was the wisdom and power needed to turn all things to "a greater good, a higher purpose, and a deeper truth."

Chase realized he truly loved The Son. He had given His life for Chase and there is no greater love. He could be trusted. Chase didn't understand all that had been al-lowed in his life. People would fail him at times, but he believed now in The Son's ability to turn things around for good. In fact, He had just done that in Colt's heart and mind! When he could not understand The Son's ways, he could trust The Son's heart. He felt a freedom and oneness with The Son that filled his very being and thrilled his new spirit! He was loved and valued. He was part of the grand and good plan of The King. And he had a peace that passed all understanding. His heart was healing. He would grow and learn, and he knew for sure now. He had a family and a home . . . forever.

Other people were on the verge of grasping The King's words. People like old Miss Everdear, Joy and Gracie, Will and Able, and Gramma and Grampa Hart. Still others would need some more time before "The Deepest Truth" of all would fully take root in their lives. People like Mr. and Mrs. Tidings, Mrs. Leary, Scout, and Faith, Hope, and Love. But everyone erupted into cheers of joy as they began to grasp, as much as each was able, the awe and wonder, the wisdom and power, of such an amazing King. For He relentlessly pursued them with a love that knew no bounds. He risked all to win their hearts forever. He daringly sought to bring them out of their blindness and into His glorious light. And He invited them into the heights and fullness of His majestic kingdom forevermore!

Together, the amazed crowd arose as one mighty throng, praising The King with a love that transcended all! Everyone was hugging Him and each other at the same time! Little Faith, Hope, and Love were grasping The King's royal robe, giggling with joy. And Constable and Constance Goforth were lifting up grateful hearts as they lifted up laughing, little children into the warm, summer sunshine.

Sage grasped Serena, hugged her tightly, kissed her warmly, and swung her 'round and 'round. They both felt dizzy with joy, as love swirled in their private, little world. When they finally dropped onto the soft grass to catch their breath, little Scout flopped down beside them for a hug, and Charity threw herself into her papa's arms . . . and kissed the little smudge on his cheek.

Mr. and Mrs. Tidings exclaimed "The Glad Tidings of Great Joy!" Joy danced gracefully among the azaleas and lilacs weaving in and around the lovely clustered blossoms, her rosy cheeks aglow with absolute peace. Faith, Hope, and Love raced from The King's side, past the shimmering waters, singing glorious hallelujahs to The Wisest and most Wonderful King . . . though it all sounded just a little off-key! And then they turned head-over-heels cartwheels in the sunshine, because they knew, that they knew, that they knew, that they were loved and accepted forever and ever . . . and ever!

Jovial and a few of his friends raced up the hill, knocking each other off balance trying to reach the top first, and then rolling back down again in the thick soft grass, grinning from ear to ear. Colt, Will, and Able waved for Chase to come over and join the three of them by the lake and he did. The three had officially decided to re-name Chase, and so they dubbed him here, now, and forevermore—Noble. Noble accepted his new name with mock solemnity and ceremony, even bowing, to indicate his acceptance. He tried to stifle a chuckle on the outside, but he secretly smiled inside, at the meaning of his new name, for he realized that that was now who he truly was.

All four of the youths were soon rollicking in the lake and in the fountains' unexpected jet bursts and misty sprays, and their carefree, hilarious antics enthralled everyone around them. Constable Goforth even called out, "Hey, Noble, come 'round to my cottage sometime soon, and I'll give you a real job to do . . . some paid work!" And Noble eagerly agreed with a loud, "Yes, Sir!"

Gramma and Grampa Hart were alternately hugging and dancing a little jig that had everyone else joining in, too! Their eyes sparkled with a joy that only they could fathom. Mrs. Leary helped the little children ride on Peaceful, and then shyly walked over to the serving tables to join the other women who welcomed her warmly. She appreciated their encouragement and then helped Serena provide tea and pastries for young and old alike.

And Colt looked up to see . . . his father walking toward him! *He's here!* thought Colt. *He made it! He chose to believe The King!* Colt walked toward him, too—man to man—and they shook hands. They looked each other straight in the eye, saying much . . . without actually speaking a word.

And then *finally!* Old Mayor Hopewell quietly walked up and sat down beside Miss Everdear. She greeted him with a sweet smile, as little, pink Lilly blushed with delight . . . and as the little, pink nose of Blessing poked out of Miss Everdear's little, pink satchel! Mayor Hopewell and Miss Everdear laughed warmly together, and many of the others saw and joined in too . . . as a dove named Divine soared high above The Kingdom of The King.

Chapter 17

The Personal Connection

His Gifts of Love and Compassion

*A*nd then it was time. The Son wanted to present Colt to The King. The two walked together as The Son helped Colt weave his way through the crowded lawn to the western edge of Delightful Waters, and to Revelation Rock, and to The King of Glory. Their eyes met and the joy and honor and deep, deep love in the eyes of The

King for Colt made him drop his gaze for a moment as his heart pounded deep within him.

Colt instantly reflected back to the moment in the noisy, village square when he had first felt drawn to turn toward The Castle . . . and The King. The King had silently spoken to him then, and Colt had truly sensed His still, small voice. He knew that now. He had been hungry and thirsty for truth and relationship, and that inner call and voice had initiated the long journey that had brought him to this moment with The King.

As Colt raised his eyes, he knew that he and The King understood one another in a way that words could not convey. The King ceremoniously reached out His powerful hand to shake Colt's. He wanted to officially welcome him into The Kingdom and commend him for his quiet leadership and solid determination. Colt's hand trembled as he humbly reached out and shook The King's hand, and his heart welled up with a joy that knew no bounds. Then The King laughed with a joy that knew no bounds as He suddenly grabbed Colt and wrapped him in a powerful, king-sized hug!

Everyone rejoiced and continued on in the happy celebration. And then it was time for The King to go to Shy. He knew right where she'd be. She sat by a babbling brook, which is actually hidden behind much of the castle, until it appears to the right of the castle and spills gently into Delightful Waters. It's actually called Brooding Brook and is filled with rocks and boulders. It is very hard for the splashing water to maneuver around all those obstacles before it can successfully reach the quiet lake. Shy was sitting on the largest boulder, alone, looking down.

The King quietly made His way to her side and lowered His mighty frame next to her fragile figure and waited. Shy's eyes were wet with tears as she stared at the waters that were trying over and over to flow forward, yet were blocked, twirling and splattering against the hard rocks. Yet she watched as the waters, time and again, eventually gathered enough momentum to splash around and over the rocks to flow freely.

Shy looked up and into the eyes of The King, and His eyes were wet with tears, too . . . for hers had been a hard journey. He gently reached out to rest His hand upon her shoulder, but she suddenly turned to Him and buried herself in His mighty chest. The King wrapped both robed arms around her completely and enveloped her in His everlasting love.

Shy hugged The King and cried. Her tears were not tears of pain though, but of release. And The King's tears were not tears of pain either, but of joy in her choice to believe Him. She was trusting in His goodness and His truth, though she did not yet understand all that life had been . . . and why.

Shy realized that she truly loved The King. She understood that she was a new creation now, that The Son lived within her, and that He was more than enough for whatever lay ahead. She felt the grief and loneliness in her soul slowly but surely ebbing away. It would take time, but she knew that her healing was assured. And she was at peace.

Shy rested in The King's embrace for a long time and then eventually turned around, still enfolded in The King's arms, but able now to watch the others. Charity was racing to keep up with Scout but he sprinted ahead and reached Freedom first. And the triplets were heading for yet another ride on Victory. (They weren't quite ready to try Freedom yet!)

Shy eventually stood up to get a better view and The King stood with her. She was still somewhat hesitant and afraid, but she was hopeful now too. She looked up into The King's kind face, finding her value in Him alone, grasped His hand, and together they slowly walked toward Joy and Gracie. Gracie was resting and Joy had just arrived with a platter of delicious treats, enough for all to enjoy. Both of the girls saw Shy coming toward them with The King, and they smiled at each other and then at Shy. And for the very first time . . . Shy smiled back.

Oh, what untold love and unspeakable joy everyone experienced receiving The King's overflowing heart full of love and reflecting it in full measure to Him and to one another! Oh, what deep, deep truths and powers were now available as they grew in knowing Him forevermore. Oh, how He listened. Oh, how He understood. Oh, how He loved! Yes, imagine what you have always longed and wished for in the most perfect person in all the world . . . and you will discover . . . it is The King of Glory.

Eventually The King motioned, and the people glanced around and realized that The Son was no longer among them. The King pointed and they all looked toward the balcony of the castle. A large, rough-hewn, wooden cross, high and lifted up, stood silhouetted against the brilliant sunlight. The King called out, "This cross is a symbol of The Son's great love, sacrifice, and death for you. It is also a reminder that you are forgiven, made new, and united with Him.

"Remember.
Rejoice.
And be at peace."

In that holy moment, the people believed and rested—by faith—in The Son's presence within them and in the peace and joy that was theirs . . . now and forevermore.

Chapter 18

The Perfect Love

His Gift of Healing

Early the next morning, Colt headed out quickly. He couldn't wait to reach The King's stables. His father would be busy tending to the morning prep and training of the horses, and Colt wanted so much to help. Just yesterday, he and his father had had an incredible reunion as everyone had enjoyed the celebration at the castle. They had talked and laughed late into the night with the other villagers—something they had never done before. It had been perfect. Colt felt that all the issues with his father had been resolved, and he was excited to begin a brand new life with a brand new father. He suddenly felt like a child again . . . trying to help his father . . . trying to gain his father's attention . . . trying to gain his father's approval. His steps slowed as he began to realize that somehow something wasn't quite right.

That's all in the past, he thought. *I let that go. Pa didn't mean to ignore me. He was very busy after Ma died. He was grieving just like I was. He did the best he could. I've forgiven him. It's all okay now.* But the feelings would not go away. In fact, they grew stronger. He pondered them carefully and then forced them from his mind as he reached the stable doors. He stepped inside and saw his father with the horses.

"Morning, Pa!" Colt called out. His father did not hear him. He was busy brushing Gallant, the largest and most powerful stallion in The King's extensive herd. He always got the extra care . . . and the extra oats . . . and the extra special attention from Colt's father. Colt watched for a moment as the huge horse responded to his father's gentle touch and tender words. Gallant nudged the man playfully and the caregiver responded with warm laughter as he caressed the huge head and brushed his mane to perfection.

Colt stared long and hard. He could not take his eyes off them. Something was gnawing at his heart, eating away at his soul, and torturing his mind. He finally forced his eyes to turn away and slumped against the stable door. He felt sick as pain imploded deep within him. He felt rejected all over again. Displaced. Ignored. Disrespected. Unloved. He turned and impulsively slammed his fist against the stable wall, and a scream—like a wounded animal—erupted from his soul that startled all the horses who reared in their stalls and neighed in alarm. But Colt bolted and was gone before his father could see who it was.

Colt ran from the stables, from the castle grounds, and from the pain that lived in those barns and walls. He ran desperately into the woods, where he could hide and be alone. That was his haven, his resting place, where he could always regroup and start again. He came to a clearing with a vista of mountain ranges before him and blindly threw himself to the ground. He was just inches from Emotion's Edge, unaware that it was a sheer cliff, plummeting thousands of feet below.

Colt lay on the rocky edge, feeling desperately alone and repeating over and over, "I have to stop these feelings. I have to make them go away! I've got to do it myself. There's no one else!" As the brilliant sunshine crested the mountain beyond, a voice gently said, "I am with you. You are not alone and you do not have to stop the feelings." Colt lay silent and still, unsure of what he had just heard. The voice whispered again, "You are never alone. I am here, with you and in you." It was The Son's voice! Colt recognized it clearly now! He sat up and looked around but could not see Him. He waited quietly but heard no more.

Slowly, he began to recount what had just happened. The terrible thoughts. The unrelenting feelings . . . and then the reminder of The Son's presence within him. He had forgotten. In the midst of his pain, he had forgotten all the truths available to him. He wondered why. The Son spoke again. "Feelings are very real . . . and very distracting. Often they do not tell you the truth. But they can reveal that something is wrong." Colt had never known or heard that before. And he realized The Son was helping him remember times in the past when his feelings had distorted circumstances and crippled his thoughts or relationships. *This was one*, he thought. The Son, though still not visible, spoke again. "You're right, Colt."

Colt's thoughts returned to the stable and his father. But Colt had a new spirit now. The old was supposed to be gone and the new was supposed to be here. But the ugly thoughts and feelings had resurfaced, haunting and hurting and wounding him deeply. He was angry! He was anxious. He was belligerent! He was broken. His feelings were controlling him and he felt helpless. "I am your wisdom," The Son said quietly.

Colt was startled as he remembered that The Son had said He was all Colt ever needed. He realized that included wisdom. "But why can't I just figure this out all by myself?" asked Colt, right out loud, feeling just a bit strange talking to The Son he could not see.

"How are you doing . . . figuring things out on your own?" questioned The Son. Colt thought about it. He'd worked hard to make friends and had succeeded well. He'd struggled a great deal trying to figure out life all on his own with his ma gone and his pa preoccupied with work, but he'd survived. He'd even managed to initiate his own apprenticeship with one of The King's scribes. Here, The Son interrupted his thoughts. "And how do you feel . . . in your soul?"

Colt was startled. He realized that though things had looked pretty successful on the outside, he was hurting desperately on the inside. He felt isolated and alone. He felt unaccepted and unacceptable, unloved and un-lovable. Again the words of The Son pierced through both his reasoning and his feelings. "I Am the Truth, Colt, and you are loved and valued and treasured—by Me—more profoundly than you will ever understand. I am your wisdom, with you and in you always, to guide and help you."

Colt slowly rose to his feet and slowly backed away from Emotion's Edge. He was amazed at the peace entering his heart that could only have come from The Son. He was loved and The Son would always be there for him. When others would falter or fail to meet his needs at times, he could steadfastly rest in the perfect abilities of The Son within him. He had not figured that out on his own. The Son had faithfully spoken it once again to his heart and mind. He was meant for relationship and The Son was showing him the way.

Colt had one more question. He hesitated but he needed to know. "What was that twisting, ugly, evil pain that assaulted me in the stables? It was, well . . . scary."

The Son replied, "Colt, it was the power of sin in you. It is in you but it is not you. It is not your spirit, it is not your soul, and it is not your body. But it is a power in you that attacks you and only I, in you, can overcome it." Colt understood. Living life with The Son within was the only way to gain victory over such a powerful enemy, and The Son would never, ever leave him or forsake him. "I want to live and move and have My being in you, joining together with you," said The Son and Colt understood what He meant.

The Son spoke once more, this time on a lighter note. "By the way, feelings will flee when your mind and heart dwell on Me." Colt smiled. He liked the phrase. It had an easy, comforting sound to it that he knew he would need in times to come. He was ready to head back now and live it out. He suddenly stopped and cringed. "I . . . I'm sorry I'm such a disappointment . . . going back to relying on myself . . . instead of You."

The Son's voice almost broke with emotion. "Oh, Colt, if only you knew how much joy you bring to My heart! I'm thrilled to watch you grow! I already know the struggles you will face. I'm not surprised and I'm not condemning you. I'm rejoicing in every victory you win . . . like this one right now!" Colt was speechless. Would he ever grasp the wonders of such amazing grace and love? His heart burst with a desire to know The Son more and more and experience life through His eyes . . . and with His heart.

As Colt began the trek back, he started to feel awkward and unworthy again. Fear and frustration did not retreat readily, and they revisited Colt more than once as he thought about facing his father. There was so much history between them. But The Son continued planting in Colt's mind the seed of, "Feelings will flee when your mind and heart dwell on Me," and as Colt's thoughts turned once and again back to the boundless love, wisdom, and presence of The Son within him, his anxious feelings subsided. In those moments, truth settled into his soul, and he entered into a peace that truly awed him.

Colt eventually reached the door of the stables once more and this time saw his father tending to the last horse in the last stall. Colt called out, "Morning, Pa," and this time his father heard him, looked up, and greeted him in return. Colt hesitated for a moment and then said, "Could I . . . could I help you with the training this morning?" His father did not speak. He looked down and then nodded his agreement. Colt reached for the harnesses but winced at the pain in his hand. His father saw Colt's badly bruised knuckles and asked about them, but this time it was Colt who looked down and remained silent. "Let me help," his father said. His voice was flat and he avoided eye contact, but his touch was gentle as he found the needed supplies and cleansed Colt's bruises, wrapping his hand in clean, protective bandaging.

"I'm sorry that happened," his father said quietly. Colt glanced up. It seemed as though his father had somehow known what had happened. The Son helped Colt to realize that He had been talking to Colt's father, helping him to understand what had happened . . . and why. The Son had been reaching out to both of them, offering insight and help . . . and hope. The Son had been accomplishing things behind the scenes that filled Colt's heart with wonder! How much higher The Son's ways were than his own. How grateful Colt was to be united with Him. Both Colt and his father were learning and growing in the truths The Son was always ready to share. Yes, it was worth the journey to experience this level of understanding and connection. And it was only the beginning.

"Thanks, Pa," Colt said. He could sense his father was pleased though no word or outward expression indicated it was so. Colt was at peace. He had identified the wrong feelings that had led to the wrong thoughts. He had a father who loved him as best as he knew how, as much as he was able . . . but no one could provide Colt with as much love as he needed and desired—except

The Great King and His Amazing Son. How wise The Son was to teach him that, wisdom he could never have learned on his own. He realized that he had found . . . perfect love. Colt smiled. He and his father headed toward the corrals together for a full day of work. It was truly a new beginning.

Chapter 19

The Missing Blessing

His Gift of Understanding

*M*eanwhile, old Miss Everdear sat thoughtfully by Delightful Waters. All The King's words had been so much to take in and understand. She thought about The Son somehow living in her new spirit, and absent-mindedly got up and wandered toward the far eastern edge of the water and sat down again to contemplate the whole idea further. She set her satchel down and little Blessing suddenly scampered out and headed straight for the woods and was soon out of sight! Poor Miss Everdear! She was frantic! She cried out and scurried off as quickly as her frail, little legs would carry her calling, "Blessing, come back! Oh, dear, dear, dear . . . Blessing, come back!"

No one noticed as little Miss Everdear hobbled and tottered onto the narrow pathway, so soon out of sight. She called and cried out for little Blessing. She climbed the pathway as best she could, calling and searching, taking one pathway to the left and then another to the right, so that she was eventually so totally out of breath and trembling, that she had to stop at a ledge to rest. She was exhausted from exertion and worry. And so was little, pink Lilly!

It was quiet there, the trees shaded her, and Miss Everdear actually felt quite comforted. She had no idea that the place was called Pity Precipice. Some sad and some stubborn thoughts quietly tiptoed into her mind, detected no objections, patted her gently, and quickly took over.

Old Miss Everdear started thinking. *After all I've done for Blessing, after all the love and care and sacrifice and provision I've made for her, she just ran off and left me!* "Ungrateful little Missy!" old Miss Everdear complained right out loud. "Here I was so happy and look what she's done to me! I can't be running after her like this! Doesn't she know how old I am? What was she thinking, running off like that? For goodness sake, how am I ever going to find my way back now? Why haven't they come to help me? What's the matter with all those people? Don't they know how old I am? I don't have the strength for this. I don't have the time for this! I don't think anyone is concerned about me at all! And where is that Mayor anyway—when I *really* need him? The old goat! Doesn't he know how old I am? Doesn't anyone care?"

At that moment, she heard a rustle beside her and realized The Son was with her. "Oh, I'm *so* glad You're here! I didn't think I'd ever *see* You again!" And she flung her arms around Him and felt His warm embrace in return. There they sat, side by side, and old Miss Everdear cooed with happiness. "Oh, it's so good to have You here. You can fix everything and find Blessing for me, and I'll just sit right here and wait for You, and then you can carry me back to the castle!" She was *so* thrilled! He was *so* silent.

Miss Everdear looked at Him. His eyes were full of loving kindness, but He didn't say a thing and He wasn't moving anywhere or fixing anything. She sat confused for a moment and then looked down and awkwardly straightened her dress and silently wiped the mud smudge off her shoe and tucked a stray curl back under her little, lacy cap and cleared her throat several times and swung her little legs forward and backward like a small child and then looked the other way for quite a while. It was very, very quiet there.

Finally, Miss Everdear gathered all her courage, turned to The Son and whined, "You *are* going to fix everything ... *aren't* You?" The Son remained silent. Old Miss Everdear suddenly frowned. This wasn't what she had expected at all, and she started fidgeting with her fingernails. She thought back and realized she wasn't quite sure how long The Son had actually been sitting beside her ... and how much He had actually heard her say.

It was then that The Son gently spoke. "I've been here the whole time and I heard every word you said." He then brought back to her mind each crabby complaint, each self-pitying word, and each unthoughtful unkindness she had spoken.

She was shocked at her thoughts and words and behavior! Here she thought she was brand new on the inside, but just look at how she had reacted on the outside! She was mortified. She was confused. She was so upset that tears quickly flowed and rolled down her cheeks. Even little, pink Lilly shed teeny, tiny tears that splashed right on top of old Miss Everdear's tears and doubled all the trouble. They were both incredibly miserable. Old Miss Everdear could not possibly look at The Son, but He gently reached for her hand and held it tenderly in His own for a long time.

First, Miss Everdear realized that He had been loving, caring, sacrificing, and providing for her in every possible way because that's exactly Who He was. Then she thought about and grieved over losing Blessing whom she feared she'd never see again. Then she grieved over her ugly thoughts and words toward her good neighbors. And then she grieved over performing so poorly for The King and The Son. At that point, The Son quietly said, "I don't want you to perform for Me." She looked up at Him in surprise. He smiled gently and said, "My heart's desire is that you remember that I am in you, to walk with you, and to empower you when troubles and challenges come. I am your Source for all you need."

Oh dear! thought old Miss Everdear. *She had forgotten! He had said that before, but in her moment of distress, she had forgotten His presence and power and gone back to her old habits of complaining and self-pity. It was going to take time to renew her mind to the powerful new ways of The Son and her new spirit within her . . . but she was willing! He wanted to reveal His life in her each moment of the day . . . and she was willing! He wanted to join with her and give her all the grace and comfort and wisdom she needed in each circumstance . . . and oh, she was so very, very willing for Him to do so!*

This was an engaging relationship of two, not an independent, lonely journey of one. How she wanted to lean upon Him and not her own understanding. How she wanted Him to be the Author and Finisher of her faith. How she wanted to know Him more and more and the wonder of His ways. His blessings had almost escaped her, but The Son had faithfully brought them back to her understanding. Very soon she was able to whisper the words. "I'm so sorry. Please forgive me."

The Son smiled and explained, "My dear Miss Everdear, you delight my heart, and it is such a joy for Me to watch you grow! I see you acknowledging your errors. I see you desiring to do what is good. I see you realizing that you want to trust My presence and power within you moment by moment. Why, this is a wonderful victory! Forgiveness and love are already yours in abundance, and together, we will live out these truths." Miss Everdear was overwhelmed. "Oh, the height and length and breadth and depth of Your great love," she whispered. And peace flooded her soul as she rested in His arms.

Eventually Miss Everdear looked up into His eyes and asked, "What will happen now?" The Son replied gently, "It's your choice. You can stay here—on Pity Precipice—or, My dear, My desire is that you believe and rest in My presence and strength in you and begin your journey back. Will you trust Me now and will you let us begin?"

Miss Everdear didn't miss a beat. "Yes, yes I will!" she cried excitedly. She was learning—even at her age— and she smiled. Suddenly she had a thought. "Oh, oh . . . but what about Blessing?" she asked sincerely. The Son looked deeply into her eyes and replied very quietly. "Please feel free to ask of Me . . . and then trust and leave it all with Me." She looked at Him intently and understood. She nodded very slowly, and with that . . . The Son vanished. She bowed her head and asked that

Blessing would be okay, that she would come trotting up the pathway so they could return to the castle together, and then she quietly said, "Amen. So be it."

Old Miss Everdear looked hopefully toward the pathway for quite some time. While waiting, she decided that Pity Precipice was not the best place to be sitting, and she got up and stretched her little legs. But still, there was no sign of Blessing anywhere. Not even a tiny meow. She slowly straightened her cap and made sure Lilly was alright, and then, accepting His will and way—and grateful for His presence and power—she started down the path, leaving the answer in His hands.

She took slow, careful steps, acknowledging Him as she sensed Him directing her way. Here and there she would hear in her mind, *This is the way . . . turn to the right . . . now turn to the left.* It was very dark by now, and she felt quite unsteady at times, but she trusted in the One within her, and His strength came moment by moment as she continued on. Once she stumbled badly but somehow sensed His arms about her, restoring her balance, and she smiled. She was not alone. Sooner than expected, she saw the castle and scores of people with raised lanterns and torches, searching for her.

"Here I am!" she called, and Constable and Constance Goforth rushed to her side as many gathered around, asking if she was okay and was there anything they could do and wherever had she been all this time? She happily answered their questions, walking back toward the castle, and then, through the darkness, thought she saw a tiny, white puff of fluff on the top step. It moved. Her weak, old eyes blinked and peered again more intently and the crowd stared too. It moved again . . . and then it meowed! It was Blessing! She was okay! She scampered down the steps right into the arms of old Miss Everdear, who was overwhelmed with joy! Even little, pink Lilly leaned over her little, ruffled rim and kissed little Blessing.

Mayor Hopewell came hobbling through the crowd, happy to hear that Miss Everdear was safe. She smiled and said, "All is well. The Son has been with me all the way." And then, as she was carried along with the crowd, she called back, "Oh . . . by the way . . . I'm really sorry that I called you an old goat!" She was so happy . . . in so many ways!

Chapter 20

The Son Within

His Gifts of Truth and Trust

The sun rose on a new day, and Charity and Scout tried to stifle giggles. Sage and Serena were relaxing by Delightful Waters, enjoying their morning cups of creamy coffee . . . and kissing! Charity and Scout crept up behind them, intending to surprise them, but their parents suddenly whirled around and surprised them with funny growls and lots of tickles to go around.

Gramma and Grampa Hart were early risers, too, and next to arrive at the lakeside. As Gramma Hart and Serena visited, Grampa Hart asked Sage to take a walk with him around the lake. They walked slowly and chatted lightly until they were out of hearing distance from the others.

Then Grampa turned to Sage and said, "I'd like to ask you a question."

"Sure," said Sage.

Grampa Hart's brow was furrowed in thought and then he just came right out and said it. "Sage, I'd like to ask if you actually see and hear The Son like Miss Everdear and Colt described yesterday." Sage had been wondering the same thing about others. He responded quietly, "Actually, uh . . . no, I don't." Grampa Hart appeared relieved. Sage continued to shorten his steps to accommodate Grampa Hart's slower pace.

Then Sage continued. "I think The Son may choose to do that at special times in people's lives, but it probably won't be the norm. He does ask us to walk by faith, not by sight." Grampa Hart nodded and Sage thoughtfully added. "I know The Son is in me and I've experienced His communicating with me. I guess . . . I guess I would describe it as sensing impressions of His thoughts, or like a whisper in my spirit that has His imprint all over it. I don't see Him physically or hear Him audibly, but I trust Him to speak to my spirit and I believe He does."

Grampa Hart paused and then said, "I think I was believing a lie."

Sage looked over at him with a questioning look.

Grampa Hart continued. "Do you remember The King telling us that lies will trip us up?" Sage nodded. "Well, I realize I was believing a lie . . . that The Son would be there for others and speak to them, but He wouldn't be there for me or speak to me . . . especially . . . after all I'd done." Grampa looked so dejected and vulnerable, Sage gently placed his hand on his shoulder for a moment to encourage him.

Grampa Hart looked at Sage gratefully. Then he stood a little taller and sounded noticeably stronger and finished his thought. "But I can see now that that's a lie. You know, Sage, I asked The Son just this morning if He would reassure me of His presence and that He communicates with even me . . . however He desires to do so . . . and I know now He just did—through talking with you. He revealed the lie to me and replaced it with His truth." Grampa Hart smiled with relief and said, "Thank you, Sage. Thanks for listening." Sage nodded to his good friend and with that, they rounded the curve of the lake, back toward the host of people enjoying the new morning.

Mr. Tidings was the next to seek Sage's attention. He waved him over with a freshly baked apple pie in one hand and a pot of hot coffee in the other. Sage smiled and headed towards him. He was hungry. The two found a quiet spot under the oaks and dove into the pie, each wolfing down half within minutes. Then they leaned back against the oaks and sipped at their coffee.

Mr. Tidings looked concerned. Sage decided to wait for him to open up the conversation, and before long, Tidings had a question. "Sage, I'd like to ask you something. When Serena gets upset with you, what do you do?" Sage smiled. This was an easy one and he was glad to help. "Well, women like to know that you're there for them. So when Serena's sad or upset, I just hold her and she relaxes. Sometimes she cries. Sometimes she talks. And sometimes she's just silent. But she always thanks me for really caring. It just takes some time and patience, Tidings."

Mr. Tidings frowned. "It didn't work."

"What?" asked Sage.

"I tell you it didn't work. My wife was angry with me this morning, and I tried hugging her and it didn't work." Sage was stunned. Then he frowned. *What was wrong?* The impressions of The Son came to his mind. "My answer for you is often not My answer for someone else." Sage was caught off guard. He realized he was relying on his own default setting of discernment—and pride—instead of encouraging Tidings to search out The Son's solution for himself.

Whoa! He realized he had some serious unlearning to do! This was a whole new way of living life—going to The Son instead of falling back on all his old patterns.

But it was exciting, too—sensing The Son's presence and power, sensing His thoughts and answers, and enjoying the feeling of oneness he was experiencing. Sage whispered an apology to The Son and sensed His pleasure in Sage's acknowledgement and awareness of Him and His words of wisdom.

Then Sage said, "Tidings, I owe you an apology. I just blurted out my own opinion without encouraging you to listen for The Son's answer for you personally." Tidings was quiet and then mumbled, "I don't know if He'll talk to the likes of me, at least not the way He talks to you and Miss Everdear and Colt." But Sage reassured him. "He's got no favorites, Tidings. I'm telling you, He's waiting for you. Find a quiet spot and tell Him what you just told me." Mr. Tidings was unconvinced and frowned, but he promised he'd go, and he trudged toward Brooding Brook.

Charity came running over at that moment and plopped into her papa's lap, and Sage held her gently as she sighed happily. *Just like her mother*, Sage thought and smiled. Charity had a thoughtful look on her face and Sage asked what it meant. Charity confided, "Well, I was just learning from The Son this morning that He would like me to keep Shy company today."

"What was that?" asked Sage, not quite sure he had heard her correctly.

Charity calmly explained it to her papa the same way she would have explained it to her little brother. "Papa,

The King said He was going to teach me how to be a good friend, remember?" Sage had forgotten all about that. But he remembered it now and nodded.

Charity continued. "Well, The Son asked me this morning who might need a friend and I said 'Shy' right away. So He suggested I go over and talk to her today and invite her to Delightful Waters. I noticed she was off by herself, over by Brooding Brook part of the day yesterday, so I thought she might like some company. I know she's older than me, but . . . well . . . I'd like a big sister and I just thought she might like a little one."

Charity smiled at the thought and was willing to try. "So here I go!" she declared. "The Son promised He'd help me all day, and I can't wait to see what He does. I just love Him! Don't you?" And she gave her papa an extra hug and was gone before he could answer.

Sage was stunned. His little daughter was listening for The Son's voice each step of the way and trusting Him to guide her throughout her day. Sage was so humbled. *Out of the mouth of babes,* he thought, and then whispered, "Thank You," to The Son and felt the warmth of His smile.

Sage headed back toward the lake and saw Serena, who was with some women chatting over coffee. She waved happily before returning to her conversation. He decided to walk toward the castle steps and say hi to Joy and Gracie. They glanced up and welcomed him. "Oh Sage, we're so glad you're here. We wanted to ask you something." Sage had always been fond of both young ladies, as if they were his own daughters, and he was eager to help if he could . . . but the reminder by The Son to direct them to Him came through loud and clear and he smiled in acknowledgement.

Joy and Gracie both paused for an awkward moment, and then at Gracie's nod, Joy began. "Well, Sage, . . . let's say . . . that two young ladies . . . were both interested in the same young man. He's *very* nice, you know. Well, we . . . I mean, *they*, both want to get to know him better, but we . . . I mean, *they*, don't want it to interfere with their friendship. What should they do?"

It didn't take the wisdom of a sage to figure out what Joy was actually asking, and he smiled at the two lovely, young ladies who were anxiously inquiring about love and life and friendship. Sage paused for a moment and then said, "It's kind of scary, trying to figure out the future and still balance friendships you've had for years, isn't it?" They both nodded solemnly. "You're asking good questions, and it's wise to think through issues ahead of time. Life can be hard and love can be even harder to understand." At this, both young ladies suddenly blushed and looked down. Sage noticed and quickly continued. "Ah, that's why it would be good for those two ladies to go to The Son for wisdom and truth."

The young ladies looked up startled. "The Son knows what will happen in the future?"

"He sure does. He knows everything," said Sage.

"Did He know that you would marry Serena?"

It was Sage's turn now to be startled, but he gathered his thoughts quickly and said, "Why, yes, you're absolutely right. He did!" And he smiled and thanked the One who had brought them together.

"So The Son knows all about our future too?" said Joy.

"Yes, He does. So I'd encourage both of you to talk to Him about it."

Joy and Gracie looked at each other and agreed. They thanked Sage, and then suddenly realized that he knew all along that they'd been talking about themselves. They saw that quick smile and twinkle in his eye and they both relinquished a genuine, if somewhat self-conscious, grin. Then each girl headed to a quiet place to talk with The Son.

Joy picked the meadows north of the castle. But she had to cross Brooding Brook to get there, and the current was strong and carried her downstream a few times before she was able to regain her footing. Her emotions were intense. She knew what she wanted. She wanted Colt in her life and she was trying to figure out how to make that happen. She was sure The Son wanted to help her, too, so she persistently pressed on through the rapids until she reached the other side and into Meditative Meadows. It was very peaceful there, the morning breeze was warm, and a spreading oak's low-hanging branches provided a perfect resting place for her to lean against the trunk and think.

It was so strange talking to The Son when she could not see Him, but Joy steadfastly remembered the promise of His presence within her and proceeded. "You know Colt is a fine young man, a quiet leader, a strong believer in You and . . . well . . . I guess You already know how much I care for him. I know You have a plan for my life, and . . . well, I just wanted to ask your assurance that it included Colt."

It was quiet for quite some time, but eventually The Son brought some thoughts to Joy's mind. The first was from many years ago, on that *December Dream Day*, when The King had declared the kingdom's heirs for that day. She remembered Colt and Gracie, glancing shyly at each other, and then walking hand in hand from the top step of the top tower into The King's presence to be crowned "The Royal Prince and Princess of the Day." "Oh!" The word escaped from her lips involuntarily.

Then Joy recalled other times when she had seen Colt pick wildflowers on the way to school and how they had mysteriously appeared on Gracie's desk. She remembered how Colt had helped Gracie's family rebuild a portion of their home after a hard storm had damaged it. And she remembered how one day Colt had protected Gracie from Robb's bullying . . . and had a black eye the next day to prove it. Joy sat very still, pondering these memories, and then turned her head away, not wanting to accept their possible implications.

The words of The Son came gently to her mind reminding her that her attempts to meet her own needs in her own way would lead to wrong conclusions and wrong choices. She was confused. Could she possibly be doing that? Was she relying on herself and her own plans, trying to manipulate Colt into liking her and getting her needs in life met through him instead of seeking the wisdom and plans of The Son first?

Joy dismissed the questions and justified her actions. She was in love with Colt and he was pleasant to her, so she was sure it meant far more. She was overly eager and insistent on helping Colt, even though it did seem at times that she had embarrassed him. She even explained away Colt's long-standing preference and clear intentions toward Gracie, trying to distract him and redirect his attentions toward her, which she now recalled had actually annoyed him.

Joy slowly began to see more and more of the truth as The Son brought it to light. Her thoughts had been skewed. Her motives had been self-focused. And her actions had been dishonoring to all three of them. Joy felt The Son's gentle presence comfort her in the midst of each uncomfortable revelation. And eventually she humbly began to see with new eyes the actuality of her circumstances and of the relationships.

As she rested in those moments in the meadow, her intense feelings and keen disappointment slowly but surely began to subside . . . which surprised her enormously. She did want Colt to be happy. She sincerely wanted Gracie to be happy, too. And she knew the ways of The King were always right and good. She was eventually able to confess to The Son, "I do want Your will, Your way."

It was strange she had not seen all this before. How blind she had been and wondered what other things in her life she was also unaware of. It gave her cause for concern but she released them, knowing The Son would faithfully be there each time to guide, comfort, and love her each step of the way. Her feelings for Colt continued to fade and she began to reach a point of real peace. The Son was ministering grace to her in her very soul and His power within her amazed her. She trusted Him and rested in His plans and His best for all of them, and that was enough.

The Son whispered, "I do indeed have a very special plan for you, Joy, a plan to do you good all the days of your life." It was a powerful moment she would always remember, and she was actually able to smile and rest in His faithful promise to her. She breathed in the lovely fragrances, and the fresh air revitalized her as she relaxed in the beauty of the day all around her.

The quietness was eventually interrupted by someone calling her name. She turned to see Will walking toward her, waving an excited greeting, and calling out, "Good morning, Joy! I just found a series of beautiful waterfalls beyond this meadow, and I was, well, wondering if you'd like me to show them to you?"

Will was tall, strong, optimistic, and adventurous, just like she was. And he had a charming smile that caught her by surprise. Why had she not noticed it before? She smiled and nodded and started walking toward him. She really did want to join him and see the beauty of the new adventure he was offering. And The Son smiled.

Chapter 21

The Ultimate Gift

His Gifts of Living and Learning, Loving and Life!

Soon Mr. Tidings saw Sage resting on the castle steps and strode over with a quick step and the biggest grin Sage had ever recalled. Sage couldn't wait to hear what happened. "I have such good news!" said Mr. Tidings, unable to conceal his joy. "I asked The Son why my wife was so mad at me, and He didn't say a word but, in the quiet, some images came to my mind about my wife. I saw how I had dumped all the inn's bookkeeping responsibilities on her even though she wasn't very good with numbers—because I couldn't be bothered.

"And then I saw how I'd left her to deal with our children's needs, too. I didn't want to take the time and effort to sort through their arguments or listen to their day or help with their problems. I yelled at my wife to fix everything and I went fishing! I can't believe I did that!

"And then I saw how she was tired and discouraged and how I had just left her all alone to deal with it herself. The Son even showed me a secret place where she goes to cry." Here he was very quiet and it was painfully clear that he realized how much he had wounded her. Suddenly he called out, "No wonder she didn't want me to hug her! She wasn't feeling loved at all!" Sage had all he could do not to laugh right out loud. The Son sure had gotten through to Tidings.

Mr. Tidings continued, "Now here's the most amazing part of all. I told The Son what a sorry, rotten, no-good excuse for a husband I was and that I was turning over a new leaf," and that's when He said, 'I don't want you to turn over a new leaf. That's self-effort. Instead, I'd like you to' . . . how did He say it? He said He wanted me to 'renew my mind,' to believe that I am a pure, new man and that He wants to live in me and give me all the strength and patience and joy I need to love my family well. Imagine that! Isn't it amazing?" And he was giddy with the obvious joy of truth filling his soul. He really was a new man. He really had heard The Son's voice, and He sincerely wanted to start living in those truths.

"Well, I got some lovin' to do!" he said with a wink and headed off, but suddenly he stopped and turned and restated that. "I mean, The Son in me is going to live in me and we are going to go love Cookie with a love that has no bounds!" He suddenly stared at Sage. "Oh no! I just told you my pet name for my wife and she doesn't want anyone to know! Don't tell anyone, okay?" Sage nodded a solemn promise, and with that, Mr. Tidings, unable to conceal his joy, threw his hat high into the clear blue sky, and kicked his heels, which for his size, was quite a feat! And The Son smiled.

Sometime later, Joy met up with Gracie and was curious to know what The Son had revealed to her. "Nothing," said Gracie, visibly disappointed. "He was silent, and I waited quite a while to hear any words or thoughts He might share." Before Gracie had a chance to ask what The Son might have shared with her, Joy quickly said, "Well, I believe with all my heart that He will show us all in good time. I want to trust Him and stand at the fork in the road and let Him direct our paths. He is so good! So wise in all His ways! Shall we do that?" Gracie smiled at Joy's confidence and agreed.

Together they walked on, arm in arm, as the best of friends. "By the way," said Joy, "did you know that Will wants to be a knight in shining armor in The King's army, and that he's asked me to go riding with him tomorrow?" Gracie turned to her in astonishment, and Joy laughed right out loud! And The Son smiled with a special joy . . . over Joy.

Sage was back by the oaks when little Scout suddenly came running up, jumping up and down, and asking to ride on Victory once more. An instant check in Sage's spirit prompted him to say, "No, not right now, son." Scout was impatient! He didn't have time for "No." He stomped off angrily, running in that direction anyway. Sage sensed danger and ran after Scout, caught him up in his arms, and carried the defiant, little boy back. Moments later, a roaring lion emerged from the woods. The ladies screamed and started running for the castle. The men grabbed children and started heading there, too. The lion, caught off guard by the commotion and noise, disappeared as quickly as he had appeared.

Scout's eyes were wide with fear. He turned and clung to his papa, his heart pounding wildly within him. "Oh Papa! If I had run there and you had not stopped me, that lion would have hurt me!" And he buried his face in his papa's chest and hugged him with all of his little heart. Even little Scout realized that The Son had sought to protect him by his papa's "no." Scout was so sorry. He whispered an aching apology to his papa . . . and then to The Son, who comforted his little heart within.

Sage took Scout to Serena and said he needed to be alone for a while. Sage looked visibly shaken and Serena understood. Sage headed out beyond the castle, beyond the meadows and waterfalls, and eventually came upon a place called Discerning Desert. He stopped at its edge and wept. He wept with gratitude that his son was safe. He wept that The Son had checked his spirit and warned him so clearly. And he wept with joy for the love he had for the great Son of Glory.

Gently, the unseen Son spoke to his spirit. "Sage, you bring Me so much joy. You and I are beginning a very special journey, and I have much to teach you. You have a very important role to play in this kingdom. Many people's lives depend on our constant, clear communication and many challenges will face us. But you will know a Oneness with Me that few will ever experience. Will you accept the plans I have for you?" It was a very solemn moment as Sage bowed his knee and his head and said to The Son, "I love You. I trust You. I will follow You."

Sage rested there for quite some time and then slowly rose and stood, facing the vast expanse before him. This living by faith and trusting The Son within him was going to be high adventure indeed! He felt exhilarated and intimidated at the same time. He did not know what was ahead, but He knew The Son would be with him all the way. How he wanted to grow in truly knowing Him more.

The desert wind blew upon his face and the hot sun beat upon him, but a peace that passed all understanding and a joy that knew no bounds so filled his heart to overflowing that he suddenly laughed out loud with all his heart! And the laughter of The Son joined with Sage and rang out loud and clear!

Sage stayed awhile, envisioning what his new life might be like, and then, when he turned to go, he saw Colt walking toward him. Instantly they both knew that they would share in the very important plans of The Son. Colt called out and Sage smiled and made his way back toward him. Together they talked about the upcoming adventures that awaited them, and eventually they reached the castle once again.

This world would still be confusing at times, and life would still bring both sunshine and storms. Evil had entered their world, and wrong would still tempt them at times. But their pure new spirit—their true self—was united with The Son, and victories in His truths were certain, even if it took extra time sometimes. And one day the evil would be gone forever. They trusted in The King's promise for that.

Each person began to think of loved ones and friends who had chosen to stay behind in Highland. Noble thought of his ma and pa. Charity thought of Mr. Armstrong . . . and Mrs. Leary thought of Mr. Leary. Many had already decided to return to their little village to share the wonderful Good News of The King!

They realized that life wasn't about *performing*. It was about the joy and peace of getting to know The Son *within* them, clearly recognizing His voice, responding to His love, experiencing His grace, and sharing His amazing truths with others. Knowing Him personally *inwardly*, would lead to doing what was right and good *outwardly*. They knew now that He was the Source of all goodness within them! What a message of Good News they had to share!

Suddenly Charity panicked! "Oh! Mr. King, *can* I go back to Highland? I mean, is it *okay*?" The King laughed. "Yes, Charity, by all means, return to Highland. My Son is within you wherever you go. And yes, by all means, visit Mr. Armstrong. Be patient as you listen to The Son Who will share with you what to say and do. Mr. Armstrong is hurting right now though he will not tell you so. It will take him much time to learn. He is very strong in his own self-effort still." Charity understood and would remember The King's words.

The King looked out over the people and said, "My dear people, the dangerous lion you saw, which was the enemy in disguise, and the relationship challenges you still faced while here, represent the same kinds of issues you will face back in the village and in the future. Remember, there are two basic reasons why you fall back into wrong choices. You either believe a lie or you try to meet your needs yourself. Listen for The Son to guide you into the way, the truth, and the life for that is who He is. He loves you and He can show you how to love one another. And be of good courage for He has overcome all and is with you always!"

The people cheered with "Hosannas!" and "Glory Hallelujahs!" that rang throughout the beautiful kingdom! What a fascinating, new beginning, what a brand, new world, what an extraordinary, new adventure of faith this would be! Everyone celebrated and there was heard throughout the land these amazingly wonderful words:

> "Oh, how great are the gifts
> of the Great King of Glory!
> For the glory of Glory's a prize!
> But oh, how much greater
> and grander and glorious
> is the truth of His Son *in* our lives!
>
> And the great cloud of witnesses
> sang hosannas and praises,
> 'till the sun set and rose up again.
> And great were the thanks
> and the joy and rejoicing
> of the people of Glory! Amen!

. . . Oh . . . and the stolen gift, now lying beneath the ground, back in the deep, dark woods? What was inside it? Nothing. Nothing!?! Nothing. There was nothing inside the box at all. The all-wise King had not withheld or hidden anything from His precious people. He had given every good and perfect gift to

His beloved ones. And He had simply offered to them the most wonderful choice in all the world . . . the opportunity to trust and love Him in return . . .

as The Wisest Giver of all!

APPENDIX A
The Gift of Forgiveness

Hi, my friend. I'd like to share with you three clear steps to becoming a Christian.

The first step is simply to agree with God that you have done wrong things that hurt you and hurt other people. That truth is found in the Bible in a section called Romans, chapter 3, verse 23.

The second step is to realize God's decision that the penalty for sin is death. That's in Romans, chapter 6, verse 23. That is a strong statement, but remember, God has an amazing plan of grace for you.

The third step is to believe and trust the God of the Bible. Let Him know that you're sorry for your wrong ways and bad choices. Tell Him you want to repent and turn away from whatever you are trusting in instead of Him. Share with Him that you accept Jesus Christ as your Rescuer from your sins, that you believe Jesus died in your place to pay your death penalty for you. That's 1 John 1:9.

Then just thank Him for rescuing you, for wanting to have a loving relationship with you, for giving you a new spirit—a new identity—and for coming to live in you. Then rejoice and sing Hallelujah! Praise Him for His amazing love and grace to rescue you . . . yes *you*! He didn't have to help you. He wanted to help you! Because

He is great and glorious and good . . . and He loves *you* very, very much. And that's John chapter 3, verse 16.

It's that simple, and it is the most important decision you will ever make in your entire life. It is a decision that will affect you for all eternity. I pray and trust you will make that decision with God today. He wants everyone to know Him, which is 1 Timothy 2:4.

God bless you and keep you, dear friend. DD

APPENDIX B
The Gift of Connection

The presence of Christ within is indeed a mystery. Perhaps the best explanation for the writing of *The Wisest Giver* is the wonder and adventure of such a truth and a desire to share such treasure with you. The Gospels share so clearly how Jesus lived and loved and, as people, we can identify with Him. He is alive. He is real. And we can personally relate to His thoughts and feelings and interactions with others.

God, through Jesus Christ, provided for us to see divinity in human form interacting with hurting humanity. We see Jesus' divine-human compassion for the blind man and the woman at the well. We see Jesus' divine-human wisdom in His interactions with the Pharisees and the rich young ruler. And we see Jesus' divine-human mercy and grace on the cross when He whispered, "Forgive them . . . for they know not what they do."

That is what living, holy-life power looks like, and when we accept Jesus Christ as Rescuer, God implants that Jesus-life into our new spirit. Living. Loving. Caring. Giving. Sharing . . . Amazing.

God in His wisdom wants us to know that, as believers, Jesus Christ is within us, encouraging, empowering, and understanding us each and every step of our earthly journey as we interact with others and participate with Him in this life here and how. Next to the wonder of salvation itself, I have found the truth of my new identity and the presence of Christ within me to be the most comforting truths in all of Scripture. Holy Jesus, as wholly God, dwells within me now and forevermore. I am not alone. Glory to God in the highest and peace on earth to you.

Blessings, DD

The Gift of a New Spirit for Every Believer

Hi, my friend. God shares that we are three-part beings. We are body (physical), soul (our personality including our mind, will, and emotions), and spirit (our true identity). First Thessalonians 5:23 mentions we are body, soul, and spirit, and Hebrews 4:12 mentions how God's Word can divide between our soul and spirit, enabling us to grow and better understand His deeper truths.

When people believe and become Christians, their old spirit—their old identity— dies. And God then gives them a new, pure spirit as their <u>new, true, eternal identity</u>. Many Bible verses share this truth, and the following quotes are from The Large Print Amplified Bible – 1987. Parentheses and brackets were removed to simplify the reading, and some commas were added to help with clarity. The underlines were added by me for emphasis.

A person's old spirit died the moment he or she accepted Jesus as Forgiver and Rescuer. Romans 6:6 says, "We know that <u>our old unrenewed self was nailed to the cross</u> with Him . . . " which refers to Jesus, and Galatians 2:20 says, "<u>I have been crucified </u>with Christ. . . . "

A believer is then given a pure new spirit that is holy and good forever. In 2 Corinthians 5:17, God says, "Therefore, if any person is ingrafted in Christ the Messiah he is a <u>new creation, a new creature altogether;</u> the old previous moral and spiritual condition has passed away. Behold, the fresh and new has come!" John 3:3, 6 says a person must be " . . . born again . . . What is born of, from, the flesh is flesh, of the physical, is physical; and <u>what is born of the Spirit is spirit</u>." And 1 Peter 1:3 says that by God's ". . . boundless mercy we have been <u>born again</u> to an ever-living hope through the resurrection of Jesus Christ from the dead."

Other verses confirming our pure, new spirit identity include Colossians 3:9-10 that says " . . . you have stripped off the <u>old, unregenerate self</u> with its evil practice, And have clothed yourselves with <u>the new spiritual self</u> . . . " and Acts 26:18 says believers " . . . are <u>consecrated and purified</u> by faith in Me," again referring to Jesus.

This is so very important that God continues to give us verse after verse to help us understand how real our new identity is to our understanding, growth, and security. *Identity is determined by birth, not performance.* So first we are born physically as sinners.

Then God shares in Romans 3:26 that when we are born a second time, spiritually, He "<u>justifies and accepts as righteous</u> him who has true faith in Jesus." Romans 4:25 says Jesus ". . . was betrayed and put to death because of our misdeeds <u>and was raised to secure our justification,</u> our acquittal, making our account balance and <u>absolving us from all guilt before God</u>." And 1 Corinthians 1:2 calls believers " . . . consecrated and <u>purified and made holy in Christ Jesus.</u> . . . " Even Romans 8:1 says,

"Therefore, there is now <u>no condemnation, no adjudging guilty of wrongs, for those who are in Christ Jesus.</u>" Now that is amazing!

But God is not finished revealing the fullness of this vital truth. He wants us as Christians to be settled and grounded forever in the beautiful, new identity spirit He has given us forever! So He continues to add Colossians 3:12. It says believers are " . . . <u>purified and holy and well beloved by God Himself.</u> . . . " God encourages us to receive our new identity from Him, receive His presence within us, and receive His power to enable us to sincerely give mercy and kindness because that is who we truly are. Our doing something good now may look the same to others on the outside, but to us, this truth will totally transform our thinking and living and, I promise you, it is as amazing and freeing as forgiveness itself!

Not convinced of your pure, new identity yet? I totally understand. It took me almost two decades to grasp. So let's look at some more verses like Hebrews 1:3. It says this about Jesus: ". . . When He had by offering Himself accomplished <u>our cleansing of sins and riddance of guilt,</u> He sat down at the right hand of the divine Majesty on high." Hebrews 10:10 says, " . . . we <u>have been made holy, consecrated and sanctified,</u> through the offering <u>made once for all of the body of Jesus Christ, the Anointed One.</u>" And Hebrews 10:14 says regarding Jesus, "For by <u>a single offering</u> He has <u>forever completely cleansed and perfected those who are consecrated and made holy.</u>"

In contrast, Hebrews 9:9, referring to the Old Testament temple states, " . . . In it gifts and sacrifices are offered and yet are incapable of perfecting the conscience or of <u>cleansing and renewing the inner man</u> of the worshiper." Only Christ can perfect and cleanse and make our inner man brand new. And precious John, the beloved disciple, says about worshipers, in John 4:24, " . . . those who worship Him must worship Him <u>in spirit and in truth.</u> . . . "

Romans 7:15-25 is a powerful passage of Scripture revealing that the Christian's new and true desire is pure and good. However, there is a law or power called sin that is <u>in us</u> but it is <u>not us</u>. It is not our identity. This is pivotal. If you think you're a sinner in your innermost identity, you will think you cannot help but live like one, but if you know you are a pure new spirit with Christ living in you, you will much more successfully live like the new creation God says you are.

Romans 7:25 says a Christian wants to follow God, to love Him and love others, but our flesh, which is our old pattern of living life, wants to follow the law or power of sin. That is the dilemma. The conflict is not you against yourself. The conflict is your new spirit identity against the law or power of sin within you. So the question is: will you believe your new identity based on God's Word, or will you continue to believe your old identity based on your behavior? Will you believe God that you are new and that Christ lives in you and empowers you, or will you succumb to your old ways of thinking, your old ways of living, and try in self-effort to meet your own needs in your own way? That is a performance-based way of life, not a grace-based way of life, and it leads to defeat and discouragement over and over again. I think you know exactly what I mean.

So let's take a look at this with a practical example. If you studied and became a surgeon, you have the degree, the certification, and the ID badge that gets you into the surgical unit. Your ID proves who you are. You walk into surgery and you perform the operation . . . because that is who you are. (I'd never get past the front door security! I don't have the right ID.)

Or, let's say you went to the police academy and graduated. You have the diploma, the badge, and your ID, and you accept a new position at a police station. You now have the authority to investigate crime scenes. You can stop traffic and redirect it. You can arrest a suspect. You carry out your responsibilities and job because that's who you are. (They'd arrest me in a heartbeat for trying to do any of those things. I'm not a police officer. I don't have the ID.)

In the same way, if you know God has made you brand new on the inside, if you know you have a new ID, if you believe Christ actually lives in you and empowers you to live in God's ways, you will far more often win the battle and do what is right. It's who you are. When you do sin now, it won't be because your identity is a sinner. It will often be because Satan has deceived you with a lie and God wants to reveal the truth to you. Or it may be you are trying in self-effort to get your own needs met your own way, but God wants to show you how He will meet your every need in His way. (Now I'll admit that's a roller coaster ride if there ever was one, but it's worth every victory you two win together!)

Again, *behavior does not determine identity.* Believers can do wrong things, and unbelievers can accomplish some good but temporary things. *It is birth that determines your eternal identity.* First, people are born physically as sinners. That is their identity. That is their broken spirit. But when someone becomes a Christian—when they accept Christ as Rescuer and Forgiver and Savior—they are born again, born a second time, born spiritually with a brand new, pure spirit, and now that is their wonderful, new eternal identity!

It is God's heart and desire for you to understand these truths and be born a second time so you can know your new identity! It sets you free! It empowers you with the life of Christ within you! And it affects the rest of the way you live your life. You'll either struggle on to perform in self-effort, or you will live in your new, pure identity with His power and abilities in you to move through the challenges and changes of your life. It is your choice, my friend. I pray His truths fill your heart and soul with everlasting joy!

Blessings, DD

APPENDIX D
The Gift of Christ Living in Every Believer

The Power Source of all power sources is here! And He's in every believer! His name is Jesus Christ! Here's a beautifully clear verse that helps us understand. Galatians 2:20 says, "I have been crucified with Christ, in Him I have shared His crucifixion; it is no longer I who live, but <u>Christ the Messiah lives in me;</u> and the life I now live in the body, I live by faith in, by adherence to and reliance on and complete trust in, The Son of God, Who loved me and gave Himself up for me." Paul says in Galatians 1:15-16 that God " . . . called me by His grace . . . to reveal, unveil, disclose <u>His Son within me</u>. . . . " Christ joins with our new spirit and together we accomplish good works by His power. It is not our self-effort. It's His life within us that enables us to do good things.

Okay, this is new and hard to grasp. I understand. I've been there. So let's head on to some more amazing truths to help us out. (God's got all the verses you need . . . just for you . . . and His desire is for you to understand all of His amazing grace.) Ephesians 6:10 says, "In conclusion, be strong in the Lord, <u>be empowered through your union with Him, draw your strength from Him, that strength which His boundless might provides.</u>" He's the Power Supply. We get to participate with Him. Sounds like a great deal to me! Philippians

2:13 also says, "<u>Not in your own strength</u>, for it is <u>God Who is all the while effectually at work in you, energizing and creating in you the power and desire,</u> both to will and to work for His good pleasure.... " This is one of my personal favorites and has carried me through many challenging times. I couldn't do it but His power in me carried me through. His life in me carried me through. It's simply amazing. It'll make you cry with joy when you grasp it.

Let's close with a few more verses. Romans 8:10 says that if you're a believer, "<u>Christ lives in you</u>" and your "spirit is alive because of the righteousness that He imputes to you." And Colossians 1:27 talks about " . . . this mystery which is <u>Christ within and among you. . . . </u>" Believe Him. He's got the monopoly on truth and He tells you the truth to win your heart forever! What an amazing plan God has designed!

By the way, God gives us new names when we decide to believe Him. He's officially declaring outwardly what has already happened to us inwardly. In John 1:12 and Romans 8:16, He calls us "<u>children of God</u>." In 1 Corinthians 1:2 (and dozens of other places), He calls us "<u>saints</u>." (Wow, that's a shocker, isn't it!) And in John 10:27, Jesus calls us "<u>sheep</u>" who hear His voice and follow Him. We are loved, dear friend. Dearly loved. It's rock-solid. It's real. And it's eternal and forever.

So let's do a quick review. If you have accepted Jesus Christ as your Rescuer and Savior, you are forgiven and your old spirit has died. God has now given you a pure new spirit and identity, and that is who you really are, now and forevermore. That's amazing all on its own! But there's more! Christ has come to dwell in your new spirit, to love you and empower you and live His perfect life within you. May His truths renew your mind and fill your heart with the eternal joy and peace only He can give to His precious, dearly loved people.

• • • • •

If you'd like to know more about new life in Christ, check out the following authors and websites:

AndrewFarley.org
Operation220.org
Pete Briscoe – Amazon.com
Abundantlivingresources.org
June Hunt – hopefortheheart.org
Tony Evans – Amazon.com
Dr. Charles Stanley – InTouch.org

God bless you. DD

The Gift of Questions and Discovery

The power of allegory was mentioned at the start of our journey together, and that secret, second story weaves its way deeply and surely within this story of Colt, Miss Everdear, and Sage. Let's look into that amazing, second, spiritual world to discover the amazing biblical truths that offer forgiveness, healing, and victory in our hearts and lives. If you're reading this with family or friends, you might consider reading the question aloud and discussing it. Just cover up the answer directly below it until you're ready to read it aloud. If you're reading on your own, take a moment to read through these questions and think about your answers. God bless you as you think through these truths of life.

Chapter 1: The Perfect Kingdom

1. Why was the village of Highland such a perfect place?

    A: It gave perfect examples of perfect people and perfect relationships filled with love, joy, and peace. It revealed how The King had filled to overflowing all their needs for love, security, and purpose. It is a symbol for the Garden of Eden in the Bible and how God designed a perfect world of goodness.

2. The King and The Son are symbols for someone else. Who do you think they are?

   A: The King is God the Father, the God of the Bible, full of perfect wisdom and love. He wants us to know Him and His loving plan so we can enjoy a real relationship with Him as our perfect, powerful, loving Lord God Almighty. The Son is Jesus Christ, the Rescuer and Savior of the world.

3. Who is the most important person to you in your world and why?

   A: Answers will vary but notice how the traits you love about someone are most probably the characteristics of God Himself: kindness, gentleness, goodness, love . . . and yes, fun, joy, and laughter, too!

Chapter 2: The Summer Dream

1. What do you love most about The King and The Son?

   A: Answers will vary but it is wonderful to see how warmly and personally They interact with children and adults, just like Jesus did while on earth. The Bible shares how children loved to be with Jesus.

2. What is your idea of a perfect *Dream Day?*

   A: This is a time to dream. Let your mind soar and enjoy the wonderful gift of imagination! You'll be surprised at what might come to mind.

3. What does God think of you? Have you ever thought of God as being full of love and grace for you personally? It's true. Take a moment to dwell on His love for you.

Chapter 3: The Winter Wonderland

1. Just for fun, there are 10 animals named in *The Wisest Giver*. You have already met four. Can you guess their names? (Hint: their initials are: G, B, V, and R-P.) I'll share the other six names a little later on.

   A: Gallant (horse), Blessing (kitten), Valiant (horse), and Roly-Poly (polar bear)!

2. What do you think The Gift is?

   A: Answers will vary. You might be curious. You might just want to keep reading. Because The King is wise and good, it seems to be something important and He is asking the people to "trust Him in this matter."

3. What do you think the stranger on the silver horse might be like and why?

   A: Answers will vary. He sounds mysterious. He sounds dangerous somehow. It sounds like something is going to change soon somehow in the perfect little village.

Chapter 4: The Voluntary Decision

1. Who is the stranger on the silver horse?

A: The stranger is our enemy, Satan. He is a liar, a deceiver, and a tempter.

2. How does he manipulate the people and twist the truth?

A: He asks questions to tempt the people to doubt the goodness of The King, just like he tempted Adam and Eve in the Bible to doubt the goodness of God, and just like he tempts us today. He asked them questions like:

"Did The King tell you *not* to open it?"

"I wonder what's inside?"

"Why would such a good King *withhold* something from you?"

"Wouldn't He freely give you the greatest gift of all?"

"Surely a gift is meant to be *given.*"

"I wonder what The King is *hiding?*"

His words seem innocent. He even politely apologizes for perhaps not understanding the ways of their village. But his motives are evil, and his contempt for the villagers becomes obvious.

3. Do you think The King is hiding or withholding something and why?

A: Answers will vary. You may trust The King and defend Him and His character. You may doubt His goodness and question His motives at this point. We will see more of His character as the story unfolds.

Chapter 5: The Tragic Descent

1. Victor and Victoria are much like the biblical Adam and Eve back in the Garden of Eden. In our story, they made their own choice but they also carried out the will of all the other people in the village too, who doubted, distrusted, and disobeyed The Great King of Glory. Can you see yourself in the story? Are we each responsible for how we choose? Why?

   A: Answers will vary. Sometimes we accept responsibility for our choices. Other times we want to excuse ourselves, blame others, or deny the issues altogether. I've heard it said that, "Our response is our responsibility." God gives us free will and we are responsible for our choices. We all struggle at times to see and accept this but it is true. One of God's names is Truth.

2. How did The King counsel and warn Victor and Victoria?

   A: There were three ways: the physical obstacle of "Think Again Thicket," the emotional barrier of "Beware Again Wall," and the spiritual struggle of "Ponder Again Pond." But they refused all His guidance.

3. How did Victor and Victoria handle each struggle?

   A: At the first struggle, Victoria said, "I will . . . " leaving God out of her decision-making and Victor agreed. At the second struggle, they thought about turning back but eventually were tempted and continued to choose their own will and way. And at the third struggle, they ignored and refused to look at the issues anymore and deliberately chose self over The King, who is God.

Chapter 6: The Deadly Consequence

1. How would you describe the results of their choices?

   A: It brought evil into their world and it was never the same again. It caused pain and horror and destruction. People became separated from The King. Sin severed their relationship with Him and crippled their spirits. It changed their world forever and started the war between good and evil that we see today.

2. Can you think of examples in the story of how sin affected different people?

   A: Victor and Victoria verbally lashed out at each other. Mrs. Sharp and Mr. Crafty screamed angrily. Victor blamed the villagers for making him steal the gift instead of accepting his responsibility. They all began believing lies such as they were now unlovable, unimportant, unworthy, and unacceptable. They succumbed to pride, shame, and guilt. They blamed others, excused themselves, and denied what they had done. They also felt panic and defensiveness, all things they had never experienced before.

3. Do you think you are more like Victor or Victoria? Why is that?

A: Answers will vary. Victoria gave up, overwhelmed with pain, while Victor fought back angrily, but they both succumbed to sin.

4. Why did the author specifically use the word "fall" to describe Victoria's dropping to the ground and also Victor's collapse?

A: It is a reference to "The Fall," the term Christians use to describe the first sin.

Chapter 7: The Wisest Response

1. How did The King respond to the people's choice?

A: The King responded as God does—with grief, ever-constant love, realization of the result of sin—which is death—and a plan to rescue them as He reached out over and over again to them.

2. What were the two greatest gifts in life and what happened to them?

A. The first gift was perfect relationship with The King and sin destroyed it. The second gift was their perfect spirit, and sin crippled their spirit beyond repair.

3. How did the people treat the Great King of Glory and The Son they had known and loved for so long?

A: They responded with pride and anger, throwing stones at The King. They chose to live life apart from Him. And, in their sin, they chose to kill The Son. We see who they have become and it is devastating.

Chapter 8: The Necessary Challenge

1. What were the three problems the people faced because of the sun's absence?

A: The first was dimness. It became hard to see and understand what was happening. The second was coldness. It became hard to feel because of numbness. And the third was drought. It became hard to live when life seemed to be draining away.

Chapter 9: The Beginning Search

1. Who is your favorite character so far and why?

   A: Answers will vary. It will be interesting to see who people choose and why.

2. Why did the people turn toward the castle and The King?

   A: They realized they needed help. They turned to The King for answers. They discovered hope.

3. The quote, "Come, all who are weak and weary and weighed down," is a re-phrased reference to Matthew 11:28-29. Would you read these actual verses in the Bible and talk about what they mean?

A: These tender words are spoken by Jesus who invites all who are tired and discouraged to come to Him. He promises to *give* them rest in Him, and He promises that they will *find* rest and relief in their souls, which is again their mind, will, and emotions. It is a very comforting verse of hope and assurance of His kind compassion and presence in our lives.

Chapter 10: The Humble Journey

1. Why did some people refuse to start the journey?
   A: They refused to acknowledge their need.
2. What do the Golden Gates represent?
   A: They show that God invites and welcomes us to come to Him no matter what we have done.
3. Who is the Lover of the Lambs and the Overflowing Fountain?
   A: Jesus is called the loving Shepherd and the Living Water for each and every one of us.
4. Why did Mr. Armstrong turn back when he was such a strong man?
   A: He was strong physically in his own effort but he was weak in his spiritual choices.

Chapter 11: The Highest Truth

1. What are the two parts of "The Highest Truth?" (Hint: You can check the Table of Contents.)
   A: First, God forgives us, and, second, He

establishes a loving relationship with us. So we are forgiven and can now enjoy a loving relationship with God!

2. Let's fill in the blanks about "The Highest Truth."

First, the people chose to _____ their wrongs to The King.

Then the people chose to _____ The King to forgive them by having His Son die in their place to pay for their wrongs.

Then The King forgave the people and they gratefully _____ The King's gift, and He welcomed them into a loving relationship with Him forever!

A: admit, ask, accepted

3. Have you accepted Jesus as your Rescuer? If so, share your story with someone you care about. If you haven't accepted Jesus yet as your Rescuer and Friend, I would like to ask you to take a moment and read "The Gift of Forgiveness" (p. 181). I hope you will find it very helpful in understanding and accepting His love for you.

Chapter 12: The Spiritual Celebration

1. The people of Highland are truly celebrating God's great gifts! Can you think of other ways you'd celebrate the most important day of your life?

A: Answers will vary. Enjoy imagining!

2. How does The King show His amazing love?
   A: He jumps off the castle balcony to the lawn seven stories below to run to His beloved ones! He hugs and kisses all, swinging little ones up into the beautiful sunshine! He welcomes little ones to rest in His lap and listens to stories and jokes and little whispers children want to share. He provides a grand feast with music and joy and laughter. And He provides adventures with Victory, Freedom, and Peaceful. His gifts are abundant and full of love!
3. Did you ever wonder what had happened to Victor and Victoria?
   A: Some will have guessed their identity. Others will be totally surprised.

Chapter 13: The Deepest Truth
1. What was The King's heart's desire and why did the sun disappear?
   A. The King said, "My heart's desire was to set you free from the darkness and lies that were hurting you. I did it to encourage you to seek a truth far greater than My gifts. I did it to encourage you to seek the greatest Gift of all ... I did it to encourage you to search . . . for Me."
2. What are the two parts of "The Deepest Truth?" (Hint: You can check the Table of Contents.)
   A: The first part is that God gives us a new pure

spirit, and the second part is that Christ comes to live in us.

3. What do "The Highest Truth" and "The Deepest Truth" mean to you personally?

A: Answers will vary. Are you assured that you know Jesus Christ as Rescuer and the Lover of your heart? If not, please see "The Gift of Forgiveness" (p. 181).

Chapter 14: The Enlightening Lesson

1. Why did the Constable struggle initially to believe he was the Constable?

A: He was relying on himself and his performance, hoping to be good enough for the job.

2. Why is it a challenge to believe God when our thoughts and feelings say otherwise?

A: Our thoughts and feelings seem more real to us and we are more familiar with them. It takes time and growth to realize that God is far more real and eternal.

3. Can you share a time when God won over your thoughts and feelings?

A: Answers will vary. This is a time to celebrate!

Chapter 15: The Turning Point

1. God encourages us to be at peace because, as Christian believers, we bring Him great joy and He loves to love us. Do you believe Him? Why or

why not? What may be keeping you from accepting His love and knowing Him better?

A: Answers will vary. Listen for ways to help those who are struggling.

2. What are the three parts of your soul that the enemy attacks and how can we overcome his lies?

A: Our soul is our mind, will, and emotions. As believers, Christ lives in us, and He will help us identify the lying thoughts, the condemning feelings, and the wrong choices. He makes the Bible truths living and powerful within us.

3. How does The King describe true victory?

A: "True victory is loving others into their own victories in The Son."

Chapter 16: The Living Reality

1. What did The Son say that encouraged or comforted or helped you?

A: Answers will vary. This is a great time to encourage one another.

2. Joseph, in the Bible book called Genesis, was sold by his brothers, turned into a slave, and later thrown into prison. People lied about him. People falsely accused him. People forgot all about him. Yet he kept walking on, trusting God because he found that God was enough, and that His ways are higher and greater than any temporary, difficult circumstances. God turned those

circumstances around for good and Joseph saved millions of lives. Joseph said that people meant evil against him, but God meant it for good. Only God can turn evil around into something good. Can you think of a time in your life as a believer when God turned a problem around for good?
A: Answers will vary, but rejoice in witnessing God at work in your life!

Chapter 17: The Personal Connection
1. Describe Colt's journey and characteristics.
A: Colt had challenges in his life as we all do. Some of his characteristics are that he chose to move toward God, and he helped others to make that choice, too. He was thoughtful, spending time at his favorite spot, Contemplation Cove. He was kind, trying to help Mrs. Tidings. He was willing to be the first one to step forward to seek The King. That takes great courage, insight, and strength. His father named him well! He was not puffed up and prideful. He was at peace, believing in his new identity and The Son within him.
2. Describe Shy's journey and characteristics.
A: We don't know why Shy was shy, but she was quiet, thoughtful, and reserved. She was hesitant to spend time with Joy and Gracie. She was hesitant to start the journey. She felt unwanted and invisible. We have probably all felt that way at

times. But she, too, chose well. She moved toward healing, help, and hope.

3. Review: What are the two parts to "The Highest Truth" and what are the two parts to "The Deepest Truth?" (Hint: You can check the Table of Contents.)

   A: "The Highest Truth" is that we are forgiven and God enters into relationship with us. "The Deepest Truth" is that God gives us a new pure spirit and Christ comes to live within us. And those are gifts that last forever!

4. BONUS: What are the six named animals in these last chapters? Hint: Their initials are P, V, F, P, G, and D.

   A: Purity (lamb), Victory (buck), Freedom (eagle), Peaceful (swan), Grazer (horse), and Divine (dove)!

Chapter 18: The Perfect Love

1. Feelings can be very real at times and yet not be telling us the truth. Colt experienced that. Take a moment to think about and share how God helped you to move beyond your feelings to the truth in your situation.

   A: Answers will vary. Share in the joy of victories won!

2. When God says, "I am with you," what does that statement mean to you, and can you give an

example of how God was there for you?

A: Answers will vary, but identifying God working in our lives is pivotal to our growth and development as we interact with Him day by day. God reassures us we are not alone and that is one of the greatest comforts in life.

3. What truth did Colt realize that enabled him to forgive his dad completely?

A: Colt realized that only God could meet all his needs for love, security, and purpose. We can enjoy many wonderful relationships in life, but people will fail us at times. We need to know and walk in the truth that God meets our needs.

Chapter 19: The Missing Blessing

1. Miss Everdear used criticism and self-pity to try to get her own way. What do you do to try to get your own way and how is God helping you see that Christ living in you is best?

A: Answers will vary, but this is a time for growing and rejoicing in victories!

2. Two blessings were actually missing in Miss Everdear's life. What were they?

A: Miss Everdear's kitten, Blessing, was missing. Miss Everdear mentioned that she also almost missed the blessing of seeing The Son at work in her life.

3. What is the difference between performing in

self-effort and resting in The Son's power within you as a Christian believer?

A: It may look the same on the outside, but it is very different on the inside. It is the difference between believing and trusting in yourself and relying on your abilities to get you through life and its challenges, versus trusting that Christ is truly living within you, empowering you to live life, to forgive without retaliation, to give without thought of getting something in return, of loving, whether that love is returned or not. His life flowing through you sets you free!

Chapter 20: The Son Within

1. What lie did Grampa Hart believe and how did he overcome it?

   A: Grampa Hart thought he was unworthy to hear from The King as others had. He realized that he believed a lie. God uses many ways to help us see the lies of the enemy. He uses His Word, the Bible. He uses friends to share His truths. He is very creative in the ways He shares with us, and it is exciting to watch Him in our lives!

2. What lie did Sage believe and how did he overcome it?

   A: Sage had depended on his own insight and wisdom—the wisdom of the world—to get him through life. He realized that he needed to look to The Son for His wisdom—true wisdom—and he learned quickly and it showed in his life as he talked with others.

3. What lie did Joy believe and how did she overcome it?

A: Joy liked Colt and tried in her own self effort to get him to like her. She realized her ways were dishonoring to him, to Gracie, and to herself and hurt them all. It took time but she truly desired God's ways and the result was joy and peace.

4. When has the enemy hurt you with a lie? How did God reveal the truth to you?

A: Answers will vary. This can be a time of great discovery and victory!

Chapter 21: The Ultimate Gift

1. What is The Ultimate Gift?

A: The Ultimate Gift is God Himself giving Himself to transform our lives!

2. What are two of the basic reasons we still sin now?

A: Two main reasons we sin now as believers are because we are believing a lie, or we are still trying to meet our own needs in our own way . . . which is also a lie. Ask God to show you these areas in your life. He loves to teach and heal and win victories with you!

3. Have you accepted Jesus as your Rescuer? If so, you are forgiven and have a new relationship with God! You are also a pure new creation and Christ lives in you! And that is victory! If you have not yet accepted Jesus as your Rescuer, would you accept Him now? Please read the page called "The Gift of Forgiveness" (p. 181) to help with questions you may have.

God bless you. DD

62189667R00134

Made in the USA
Lexington, KY
05 April 2017